ELFQUEST: WOLFRIDER

VOLUME TWO

ELFQUEST CREATED BY

**WENDY &
RICHARD PINI**

ELFQUEST: WOLFRIDER

VOLUME TWO

ELFQUEST: WOLFRIDER VOLUME TWO
Published by DC Comics. Cover, compilation, timeline and character introduction copyright

Originally published in single magazine form in ELFQUEST VOL.2, NUMBER 33; ELFQUEST-BLOOD OF TEN CHIEFS #10, 11, 19; WARP GRAPHICS ANNUAL #1. Originally published in book form in ELFQUEST-IN ALL BUT BLOOD (Elfquest Reader's Collection Vol. 8a); ELFQUEST-WOLFRIDER! (Elfquest Reader's Collection Vol. 9a).

DC Comics, 1700 Broadway, New York, NY 10019
A Warner Bros. Entertainment Company
Printed in Canada. Second Printing.
ISBN: 1-4012-0132-6

QUEST: WOLFRIDER VOLUME TWO

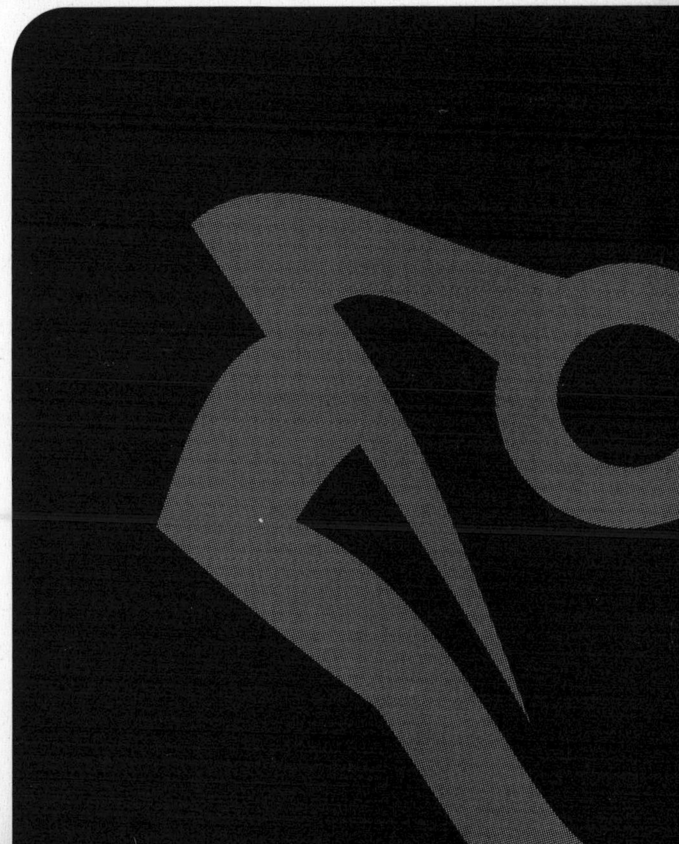

The ElfQuest Saga is an ever-unfolding story spanning countless millennia that follows the adventures of humans, trolls and various elfin tribes. Some of the events that occur prior to the time of this volume are outlined below using the very first published ElfQuest story, "Fire & Flight," as a benchmark. That tale will be released in this format in 2004.

0

1,000

2,000

3,000

4,000

5,000

6,000

7,000

8,000

9,000

10,000

2,000 - 300 YEARS BEFORE

Goodtree, eighth chief of the Wolfriders, founds a new Holt deep in the woods and creates the Father Tree where the Wolfriders can all live. Her son, *Mantricker, is* the first in several generations to have to deal with nomadic humans again.

Mantricker's son, *Bearclaw,* discovers Greymung's trolls who live in the caverns and tunnels beneath the Holt. Bearclaw becomes the Wolfriders' tenth chief.

In the distant Forbidden Grove near Blue Mountain, *Petalwing* and the preservers tirelessly protect their mysterious wrapstuff bundles.

Among the Wolfriders, *Treestump, Clearbrook, Moonshade, Strongbow, One-Eye, Redlance, Pike, Rainsong* and *Woodlock* are born.

4,000 YEARS BEFORE

Freefoot leads the Wolfriders during a prosperous time. Game is plentiful and life is easy.

Freefoot's son, Oakroot, subsequently becomes chief and later takes the name *Tanner.*

9,000 YEARS BEFORE

Wolfrider chief Timmorn feels the conflict between his elf and wolf sides, and leaves the tribe to find his own destiny. *Rahnee the She-Wolf* takes over as leader, followed by her son *Prey-Pacer.*

10,000 YEARS BEFORE

Over time, the early High Ones become too many for their faraway planet to support. Eventually groups of these beings travel into space to seek out possibilities on other worlds, bringing along trolls and preservers as helpers. *Timmain's* group discovers the World of Two Moons, but as the crystalline ship approaches, the trolls revolt. The High Ones lose control and crash-land far in the new world's past. Ape-like primitive humans greet them with brutality, and the elfin High Ones scatter into the surrounding forest.

In order to survive, Timmain magically takes on a wolf's form and hunts for the other elves. In time, the High Ones adapt, making a spartan life for themselves. *Timmorn,* first chief of the Wolfriders, is born to Timmain and a true wolf.

10,000 YEARS BEFORE

ELFQUEST: FIRE & FLIGHT VOL. 1

TIMELINE

0
475
600
1,000
2,000
3,000
4,000
5,000
6,000
7,000
8,000
9,000
10,000

425 YEARS BEFORE

The Wolfriders have known peace for years, but one day young Cutter makes a sobering discovery: the Humans have returned.

OUR STORY BEGINS HERE...

600 YEARS BEFORE

Deep in the desert to the south of the Holt, *Rayek* is born to Sun Villagers Jarrah and Ingen. *Leetah* is born to Suntoucher and Toorah twelve years later.

7,000 YEARS BEFORE

A crucial event occurs during the reign of the fourth chief of the Wolfriders: Swift-Spear goes to war for the first time against the humans of a nearby village. The humans are forced to leave, and he earns the name *Two-Spear.*

Two-Spear has strange dreams of the humans returning and believes the elves are no longer safe. He becomes obsessed by the dreams and tries repeatedly to convince the Wolfriders they must wipe out the human threat for all time. When his chieftainship is challenged by his sister *Huntress Skyfire,* the tribe splits. Two-Spear leaves with his followers, and Skyfire becomes chief of the remaining tribe.

10,000 - 8,000 YEARS BEFORE

In a long diaspora, descendants of the High Ones wander the world. *Savah* and her family settle the Sun Village in the desert at Sorrow's End. Lord Voll and the Gliders move into Blue Mountain and shut themselves away from the world.

Guttlekraw becomes king of the trolls, who have fled to the cold north.

Ekuar and two rock-shaper companions discover the abandoned palace-ship of the High Ones but are enslaved by Guttlekraw. Glaciers force the trolls to move south, tunneling under the future Holt of the Wolfriders.

Greymung rebels against Guttlekraw. Guttlekraw and his cohorts return north, and the three rock-shaper elves escape in the melee. Greymung, now king of the forest trolls, sends a scout to search for the escaped trio.

Winnowill leaves Blue Mountain, finds the troll, seduces him and gives birth to *Two-Edge.* She later kills the troll.

The ElfQuest saga spans thousands of years and to date has introduced readers to hundreds of characters. At the time of the stories in this volume, these are the major characters you will meet and get to know.

THE WOLFRIDERS

BEARCLAW

Tenth chief of the Wolfriders, Bearclaw leads the tribe in decisive fashion. Still, he prides himself in his ability to track, hunt and fight on his own, often going out solo against the tribe's better judgment. He's quick to action but is also easily tempted by dreamberry wine or gambling with the trolls. Joyleaf is the only one able to persuade him away from a course he's set.

JOYLEAF

Bearclaw's lifemate is the one elf who can channel his fiery temper and energies into something productive. Joyleaf's wisdom often has prevented the tribe from making a foolish mistake. While she loves her mate, she remains fierce in her own convictions and is a force to reckon with when her tribe or her cub Cutter are threatened.

CUTTER

While his name denotes his skill with a sword, Cutter is not a cold and merciless death-dealer. Strong in his beliefs, he will nevertheless bend even the most fundamental of them if the well-being of his tribe is at stake. Skywise believes that what sets Cutter apart from all past Wolfrider chieftains is his imagination and ability to not only accept change, but take advantage of it.

SKYWISE

Orphaned at birth, Skywise is the resident stargazer of the Wolfriders, and only his interest in elf maidens rivals his passion for understanding the mysteries of the universe. Skywise is Cutter's counselor, confidant, and closest friend. While he is capable of deep seriousness, nothing can diminish Skywise's jovial and rakish manner.

TREESTUMP

Seemingly gruff and no-nonsense, Treestump also has a vulnerable side, especially when it comes to protecting the well-being of his tribemates. More than a thousand years of living with "the Way" has given Treestump a wellspring of wisdom, allowing him to find calm even in the face of great danger. He is something of a father figure to the entire tribe.

STRONGBOW

Strongbow is the reserved, silent master archer of the Wolfriders. Ever the devil's advocate, he is often proved right but finds no value in saying "I told you so." Strongbow is extremely serious, rarely smiles, and prefers sending to audible speech. He is completely devoted to his lifemate, Moonshade, and intensely proud of their son Dart.

NIGHTFALL

Nightfall is the beautiful counterpoint to her lifemate, Redlance, and one of the most skilled hunters in the tribe. She is cool and calculated, neither vengeful nor violent unless absolutely necessary. The relationship between Nightfall and Redlance is very much one of yin and yang. Nightfall grew up with Cutter and is strongly loyal to the young chief.

REDLANCE

Redlance is the sweet-natured plantshaper of the Wolfriders. Indeed, he will only use his talents defensively to protect the tribe. Redlance is too much a pacifist at heart to do willful harm, and this gentleness makes him a natural to care for the cubs of the tribe. Redlance is a master of the soft counsel, gently prodding other, more headstrong elves in the right direction.

MOONSHADE

Moonshade is the Wolfriders' tanner. Though the process can be lengthy and tedious, she enjoys the quiet hours spent bringing the beauty out of a supple hide. Moonshade, like her lifemate Strongbow, is very much a traditionalist, strong-minded and with unshakable beliefs. Completely devoted to her mate, Moonshade will defend him even when she knows he's wrong.

SCOUTER

Scouter has the sharpest eyes of all the Wolfriders. He is steadfast, loyal, and often overprotective. He is also extremely intolerant of anyone, tribemates included, whom he perceives as putting his loved ones in jeopardy. Dewshine and Scouter have been lovemates for most of their lives, yet are not Recognized.

DEWSHINE

Dewshine, swift and graceful as a deer, is the most agile and free-spirited of the Wolfriders – and that takes some doing! She has a beautiful voice, full of melody and laughter. Song and dance are passions with her, and she has a talent for mimicking birdsong.

CLEARBROOK

Calm, dignified and thoughtful, choosing her words carefully, Clearbrook is the eldest female Wolfrider. An elder of the tribe, she advises in a quiet manner that masks the fierceness of an accomplished warrior, but her fury knows no bounds if her loved ones are threatened.

ONE-EYE

Woodhue gained his new sobriquet after his right eye was put out by humans. Needless to say, this seeded a lifelong hatred and distrust of the "five-fingers." Although he still considers Cutter a cub, One-Eye never questions Cutter's judgments; Cutter is chief and that is that. One-Eye is fierce in battle, especially when his cub, Scouter, or his lifemate, Clearbrook, is endangered.

PIKE

Pike is the Wolfriders' resident storyteller, taking his name from his preferred weapon. The most ordinary and happy-go-lucky of the Wolfriders, Pike has no grand ideals or desires for quests – he is a follower and rarely questions his chief's orders. Fully immersed in the "now of wolf thought" he clings through thick and thin to his two greatest loves: dreamberries and taking the easy path.

THE TROLLS

The trolls are the descendants of the ape-like servants of the firstcomers, who, having rebelled at their slave-like status within the palace-ship, caused the cosmic disaster that left them all stranded in the primeval, prehistoric era of the World of Two Moons. Taking to caves and tunnels beneath the land, they adapted over time to grow more massive, uglier and much greedier.

PICKNOSE

His name was inspired by his most prominent facial feature, which resembles the curved business end of a pick. The success of Picknose's interactions with the Wolfriders has been mixed at best, for while he does possess a sort of honor, he is also an opportunist of the first water.

OLD MAGGOTY

Old Maggoty was caught by Bearclaw one night stealing dreamberries near the Wolfriders' Holt. The two then became liaisons for their respective peoples in matters of trade. Old Maggoty is a master of herb lore and is renowned for brewing dreamberry wine, a potent lavender distillation that can set even the strongest-stomached elf on his pointed ear.

ODDBIT

Oddbit embodies all the troll maidenly virtues: she's greedy, deceptive, manipulative, coy, vain and fickle. She is the ultimate material girl, adorning the footstools of both King Guttlekraw and, later, King Greymung. After Picknose rescued her, Oddbit kept the lovesick troll dangling for years.

KING GUTTLEKRAW

Guttlekraw rules over the ferocious northern trolls who inhabit the caverns and tunnels surrounding the remains of the palace-like starship that brought the High Ones to the World of Two Moons. For thousands of years this merciless tyrant and his warriors have made certain that no elves can ever return to their ancestral vessel.

KING GREYMUNG

Compared to the rigors of life in the frozen north, Greymung and his forest trolls have it easy. While he may have shown some grit when he rebelled against Guttlekraw in the distant past, now Greymung has little to do but sit on his jewel-encrusted throne, mistrusting one and all in his underground kingdom.

TWO-EDGE

Two-Edge is the cunning half-troll, half-elf son of Winnowill and a troll named Smelt. An ingenious mastersmith and inventor, he is a teacher to the trolls. Like Timmorn, Two-Edge is unique on the World of Two Moons. Abused as a child by his mother, Two-Edge was devastated when she killed his father and now walks a fine line between cleverness and insanity.

IN THE PREVIOUS VOLUME

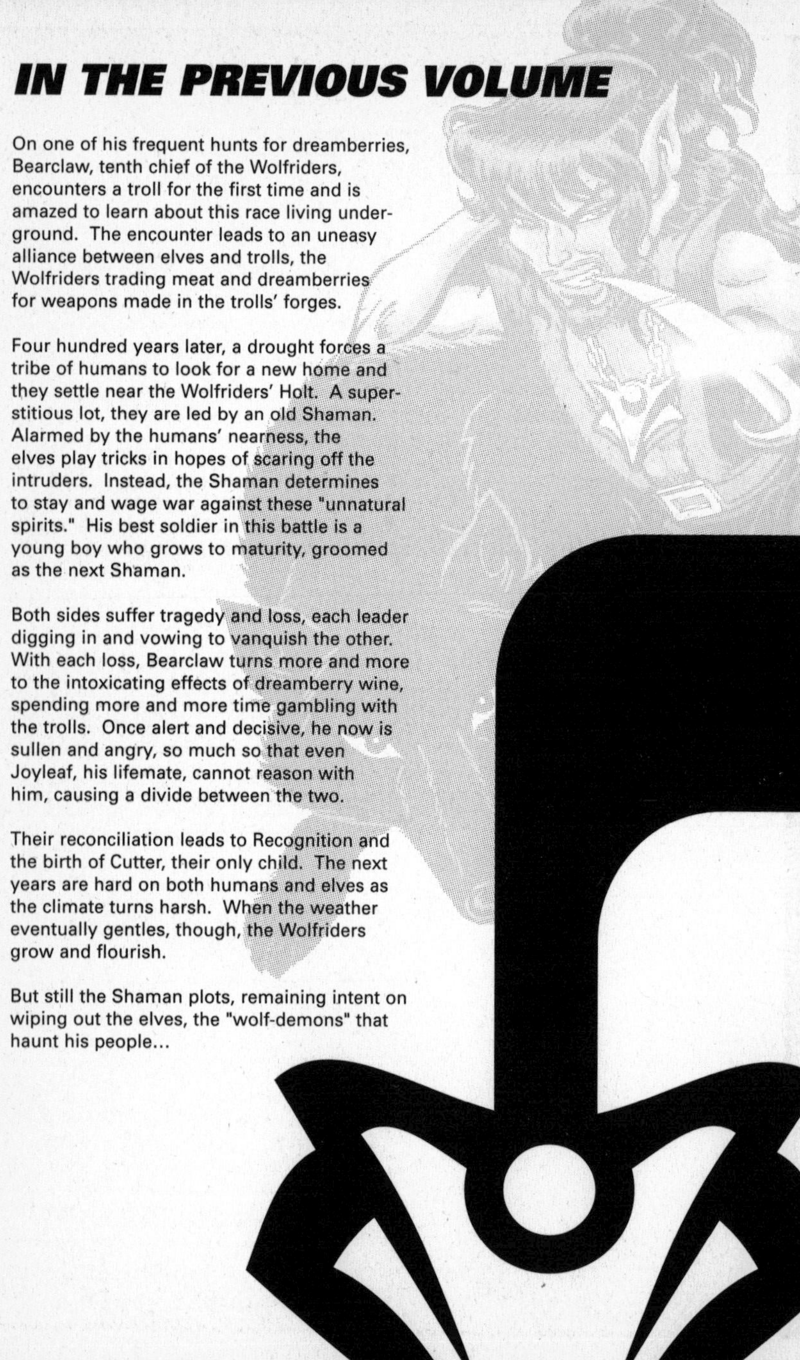

On one of his frequent hunts for dreamberries, Bearclaw, tenth chief of the Wolfriders, encounters a troll for the first time and is amazed to learn about this race living underground. The encounter leads to an uneasy alliance between elves and trolls, the Wolfriders trading meat and dreamberries for weapons made in the trolls' forges.

Four hundred years later, a drought forces a tribe of humans to look for a new home and they settle near the Wolfriders' Holt. A superstitious lot, they are led by an old Shaman. Alarmed by the humans' nearness, the elves play tricks in hopes of scaring off the intruders. Instead, the Shaman determines to stay and wage war against these "unnatural spirits." His best soldier in this battle is a young boy who grows to maturity, groomed as the next Shaman.

Both sides suffer tragedy and loss, each leader digging in and vowing to vanquish the other. With each loss, Bearclaw turns more and more to the intoxicating effects of dreamberry wine, spending more and more time gambling with the trolls. Once alert and decisive, he now is sullen and angry, so much so that even Joyleaf, his lifemate, cannot reason with him, causing a divide between the two.

Their reconciliation leads to Recognition and the birth of Cutter, their only child. The next years are hard on both humans and elves as the climate turns harsh. When the weather eventually gentles, though, the Wolfriders grow and flourish.

But still the Shaman plots, remaining intent on wiping out the elves, the "wolf-demons" that haunt his people...

CUTTER MOVES WITH SURE-FOOTED SWIFTNESS THROUGH THE FOREST. IT IS HIS TWELFTH TURN OF THE SEASONS.
ONLY THE GREATEST SKILL AND CUNNING WILL BRING HIM SUCCESS IN THIS HUNT.
MORE SILENT THAN ANY BEAST, HE KEEPS HIS KEEN, YOUNG EYES FIXED --

-- ON THE PREY: HIS ROAMING SIRE WHO IS PAYING HIS LATEST VISIT TO THE TROLLS.
I HAVE TO SEE THOSE MYSTERIOUS MUD-GRUBBERS FOR MYSELF!
HAH! WON'T BEARCLAW BE SURPRISED!
I'LL BET NONE OF THE OTHER HUNTERS COULD TRAIL HIM THIS LONG WITHOUT ALERTING HIM.
HUNH? NOW WHERE'D HE GO? HOW COULD HE --
YAAH!
WHAT ARE YOU DOING OUT HERE?
GET BACK TO THE HOLT AT ONCE!
I WANT TO SEE THE TROLLS, FATHER!
COME ON, HEH HEH! I'M OLD ENOUGH!
GO HOME. DON'T MAKE ME TELL YOU A THIRD TIME.

I WANNA SEE THE CAVES!
ARE THEY REALLY FULL OF GOLD?
DO TROLLS SMELL FUNNY?
PIKE SAYS THEY DO.
GO... BACK... NOW!
BUT WHY, FATHER? HOW COME NOBODY GETS TO GO BUT YOU?
WHOPP!
UUNH!!
NOW THE YOUTH IS SILENT... AND SILENTLY HE OBEYS --
-- FOR TEARS WOULD SHAME HIM BEFORE HIS CHIEF.

MOMENTS LATER, AS JOYLEAF SEARCHES FOR HER GROWING SON...
WHURRFF?
SNIFF *SNIFFLE*
WHIIINNE WHIIINE
OH, THE POOR CUB! I KNEW IT!
SHHH, SHADOWSHEEN. I'LL TAKE CARE OF HIM.

"HE'S HIDDEN HIMSELF AWAY... TURNED TO NIGHTRUNNER FOR COMFORT."

MMM MMM MMM *SLURP*
I J-JUST WANTED *SNIFF* TO GO WITH HIM...

WHAT'S SO B-BAD ABOUT THAT?
YOU TESTED YOUR SIRE.

BEARCLAW HAS A HEAVY HAND. I'M NOT SURE WHERE HE LEARNED IT...
...BUT HE CANNOT CHANGE HIS NATURE.
HE BELIEVES A CHIEF MUST BE STRONG, AT ANY COST.

BEARCLAW LIVES COMPLETELY IN "THE NOW" AND OFTEN FORGETS THE LESSONS OF THE PAST.

HE DOESN'T QUESTION HIS OWN ACTS. TO HIM, IT'S THE WAY.

HE IS OUR CHIEF AND MUST BE OBEYED. WHAT YOU MUST LEARN, MY SON...

...IS TO PICK YOUR FIGHTS.

BUT... HOW?

BY KNOWING WHEN IT'S TIME TO GIVE IN...

...AND WHEN IT'S WORTH THE PAIN... TO TAKE A STAND.

EVEN AS SHE SMILES AT HER OWN JEST, JOYLEAF KNOWS THAT SMILE IS PARTLY FOR HERSELF...
...FOR, AS BEARCLAW'S LIFEMATE AND OFT-TIMES CONSCIENCE, SHE HAS NEEDED TO BE STRONG-WILLED PAST STUBBORNESS, FORCEFUL PAST HER OWN TENDER NATURE.
IN THE END, SHE WONDERS, WILL HER SON TAKE AFTER ONE PARENT MORE THAN THE OTHER? OR WILL HE TRULY SURPASS BOTH OF THEM TO BECOME SOMETHING UNIQUE IN WOLFRIDER LORE?
MUCH DEPENDS, SURELY, ON THE GUIDANCE HE RECEIVES NOW...

DID WE LOSE HIM YET??
I THINK SO...
ULP! THEN AGAIN, MAYBE NOT!
RRRROOOWWWLLL!!
PANT PANT!
STARJUMPER'S GETTING WINDED.. HE CAN'T KEEP CARRYING BOTH OF US...
ALL RIGHT... THEN WE STOP RUNNING.
WHAT?! TANNER'S NEEDLES, CUTTER, HAVE YOU LOST YOUR MIND?!
NO... COME ON! WE'LL GO HIGH INSTEAD!
BUT THAT BRUTE CAN CLIMB... OH, OWL PELLETS!

RUN FAST, STARJUMPER! WE'LL FOLLOW SOON!
I HOPE...
WHRFF?

THIS IS THE LAST TIME I TAKE YOU SQUIRREL HUNTING!
SQUIRRELS?! WE'RE AFTER LARGER GAME TONIGHT!
GRRR!

YOU MEAN, IT'S AFTER US!!
SNORT!!!

NOT FOR LONG. I'M TAKING A LEAF FROM MANTRICKER'S TREE OF TRICKS. WHY GO AROUND WHEN WE CAN GO OVER...
WHA--? AH HA, I SEE! SNEAKY!

GO ON AHEAD...
NO-- YOU...
WE DON'T HAVE TIME FOR THIS-- JUMP!

RRRUUNK!
HURRY! HE'S RIGHT BEHIND US -- AND I'LL BE RIGHT BEHIND YOU!!
STUBBORN 'TIL THE END OF YOUR DAYS, SON OF BEARCLAW...
SCAVENGERS
...AND TO THE END OF MiiiiiiiNE...!

OOOOOMPF!

OOOOHH -- THAT'S ENOUGH OF THAT FOR ONE DAY...

NOW GET OVER HERE -- BEFORE I HAVE TO CUT YOU OUT OF HIS BELLY!
I'M... COMING...

OHHH ROTTEN LIMBS... WHY NOW...?
I DON'T EVER THINK ABOUT FALLING...

...UNTIL I LOOK DOWN... ULP!

CUTTER... TAM! WAKE UP!

STEADY... S-S-STEADY... JUST T-TAKE YOUR...

GRRRROOWWLLL!!
EEP! ...TIME??
OH, TIMMORN GUIDE MY FOOTSTEPS NOW!

EEEEYOOOWW!!!
I-I-I-I...

...GOT YOU!!
RRNNNN!! SNORT
I MADE IT I MADE IT I MADE IT...

THAT WAS TOO CLOSE, CUTTER -- IF YOU'D WAITED ANY LONGER...
BUT I DIDN'T. SO LET'S STOP TALKING ABOUT IT.

ALL... RIGHT... ARE YOU SURE YOU'RE...
I AM NOW. BUT I'LL BE EVEN BETTER ON THE GROUND.

SOUNDS GOOD. OL' SNORT UP THERE'LL BE AN EIGHT OF DAYS FIGURING WHERE WE WENT.

STARJUMPER! YOU NEVER WERE ONE FOR LISTENING...
...BUT THANKS FOR WAITING.

HA HA! THERE'S SOME-THING YOU DON'T SEE VERY OFTEN.
HMMM? OH, YOU MEAN...?

UH-HUH... A BEAR TREED BY AN ELF! HAW!! WAIT 'TIL BEARCLAW HEARS ABOUT THIS!

...AND I FELT HIS BREATH ON MY BACK, SO I LEAPED OUT... AND SKYWISE WAS THERE TO CATCH ME!!
THAT STUPID OL' BEAR IS PROBABLY STILL UP THAT TREE ...
HAWW! I'LL WAGER YOU'RE RIGHT!
HMM-HMMMMMM...
UH, CUTTER EXAGGERATES... THERE WAS REALLY NO DANGER...
NONE AT ALL??
WELL. MAYBE A LITTLE...
GOOD! EXCITEMENT IS LIFE, CUB! KEEPS AN ELF SHARP! PUTS THE POINT IN HIS EAR!
AND HOW DID THE BEAR COME TO BE CHASING YOU? WERE YOU SNIFFING AROUND HIS DEN?
NO! YOU TOLD ME NEVER TO GO THERE.
AND YOU LISTEN SO WELL...
HE JUST GOT MAD BECAUSE WE BEAT HIM TO A NEW STINGER NEST, AND...

FRESH HONEY!!! LIFEMATE-- LOOK WHAT OUR SON HAS BROUGHT ME!
ERRRR, I MEAN, US!
I HADN'T NOTICED THAT.
YOU'VE MADE YOUR CHIEF VERY HAPPY!
...AND YOUR MOTHER VERY UNHAPPY AT THE RISK YOU TOOK!
BUT-- BUT...
IT'S REALLY DELICIOUS... WORTH A LITTLE DANGER...?
SAY USEFUL WORDS--OR NONE AT ALL!
UMF ...JOYLEAF SPEAKS TRUE. THINK OF HOW SOUR THIS SMAK WOULD TASTE HAD YOU BEEN HURT.
AS THE CHIEF'S SON, YOU NEED TO SET A BETTER EXAMPLE...
SQUISH

WHAT ABOUT THE TIME YOU SAID YOU SNUCK INTO OLD MAGGOTY'S ...
AHEM!! WELL, THAT WAS...
OR WHEN YOU DUG THAT HOLE FOR A TRAP AND FORGOT WHERE IT WAS...
THAT WAS MANY TURNS AGO... I CAN'T KEEP UP WITH EVERYTHING ...
OR THE TIME YOU PUT SAP ON THAT OLD HUMAN'S PR...
ENOUGH! THIS IS NOT ABOUT ME!
BESIDES, I'D BEEN IN THE DREAMBERRIES THAT NIGHT...
DO YOU WANT TO TRY TEACHING HIM DISCIPLINE?
SNICKER
YOUR FATHER IS TRYING -- VERY HARD GIGGLE -- TO SAY THAT THERE IS NOTHING WRONG WITH ADVEN-TURE...
...BUT JUST BE CAREFUL. THERE ARE FAR LESS RISKY THINGS FOR YOU TWO TO DO.
I KNOW! IT'S PERFECT FOR BORED CUBS! A DIGGER HUNT!

TROLL DUNG! NO SON OF MINE SCRABBLES IN THE DIRT LIKE SOME-FOUL SMELLING...
NO NO NO, MY CHIEF -- HEH HEH -- IT'S NOT *THAT* KIND OF HUNT. I'M THINKING OF A GAME THAT JOYLEAF AND I USED TO PLAY WHEN WE WERE CUBS...
YES! I REMEMBER! THAT WOULD BE PERFECT!

WE WILL COME UP WITH A LIST OF THINGS FOR THESE SCAMPS TO FIND. WE CAN GIVE THEM ANYTHING -- BUGS, BERRIES, BRANCHES ...
BA-BAH!

...BEAR FUR, HEH HEH...
TREESTUMP...
THE TRICK IS TO FIND *EVERYTHING* ON THE LIST -- BEFORE WE ALL GROW TOO OLD.

AND I GET TO DECIDE WHAT THEY LOOK FOR -- AS CHIEF AND FATHER, OF COURSE.
UH-OH...

HAW HAWW! A WONDERFUL IDEA! WISH I'D THOUGHT OF IT...
CUTTER...?
YES?
I THINK WE WERE BETTER OFF WITH THE BEAR...

THE NEXT DAY...
SIIIIGGGHHH
HOW LONG CAN IT TAKE THEM TO DECIDE WHAT WE'RE TO HUNT?
TOO LONG.
KER-PLUNK!!
I WISH THEY'D HURRY. I DON'T LIKE WAITING.
I CAN SEE...
I HOPE IT'S NOT SCREAMER BIRD EGGS...
BUT THEY DO TASTE GOOD... EH?
ARE YOU READY, MY BRAVE HUNTERS?
UH... OF COURSE! UM... WHAT HAVE YOU...?

THIS CAN BE NO ORDINARY QUEST FOR ELVES AS CLEVER AS YOU TWO. YOU'LL NEED SKILL AND LUCK -- AND THE ABILITY TO SEE BENEATH THE SURFACE OF THINGS.
YOU MUST BRING BACK A GREEN DREAM-BERRY...
...A SLIVER OF MOONLIGHT...
...AND A FOUR-FINGERED PAWFLOWER. AND YOU MUST DO THIS BEFORE THE MOONS RISE AGAIN TOMORROW NIGHT.
THINK YOU CAN?
AWW. THAT'S FOR NEWBORNS!
UMMM... WE'LL BE BACK, JOYLEAF...
WHAT'S THE HURRY? ALL SHE WANTS IS SOME BERRIES AND FLOWERS...
GREEN DREAMBERRIES! FOUR-FINGERED PAWFLOWERS! WHEN'S THE LAST TIME YOU SAW EITHER OF THOSE??

UMMM. HMM. NOT IN A LONG TIME...
HOW ABOUT "NEVER"?
GREEN DREAMBERRIES ARE RARE -- EVEN WHEN THEY'RE NOT IN SEASON -- AND IT DOESN'T MATTER ANYWAY BECAUSE I DON'T KNOW WHERE THERE ARE ANY DREAMBERRY BUSHES!
AND WHAT IS THIS ABOUT A SLIVER OF MOONLIGHT? MY KNIFE ISN'T SHARP ENOUGH TO CUT THE AIR...
MINE NEITHER, BUT I KNOW WHERE WE'LL FIND A FOUR-FINGERED PAWFLOWER...
"... IN MORNING MEADOW!"
FOUND ONE YET? I'VE LOOKED UNTIL MY FINGERS ARE AS BLUE AS THESE STUPID FLOWERS. YOU?
NO... AND I'VE BEEN ON MY KNEES SO LONG I'M STARTING TO THINK I'M A WET-NOSED GRASS-EATER...

BY THE SACRED SINGING OF THE HIGH ONES, THIS IS IMPOSSIBLE!
DEALING WITH THE BEAR WAS EASIER...

I BET WE COULD COME UP WITH A MUCH BETTER LIST.
MMMPH. PROBABLY...

SO...? YOU FIRST.
I ALWAYS GO FIRST.
THAT'S BECAUSE YOU'RE SO GOOD AT IT, OLDER "BROTHER"...

I'M NOT THAT MUCH OLDER-- JUST MORE LEVEL-HEADED.
YOU MEAN FLAT HEADED...

I'LL FLATTEN YOU, PUP OF BEARCLAW...!
HA HAA!!

SO HAVE YOU COME UP WITH ANOTHER LIST YET?

I'VE GOT IT-- AND YOU GAVE THE HINT! GO GET THE ***TROLL-WART*** OF PICKNOSE'S NOSE!

EGGHHK!

HEY, YOU EVER WONDER IF HE'S GOT THEM ANYWHERE ELSE?

UGGGH!

ICK!

FORGET I ASKED...

HAIL, CUBS!
HEY, PIKE! HOW ARE YOU THIS NIGHT?

NEVER BEEN ‹HIC!› BETTER! WHAT'CHA DOING OUT HERE?
UHH -- LOOKING FOR A FOUR-FINGERED PAWFLOWER.
AND A SLIVER OF MOONLIGHT. AND A GREEN DREAM-BERRY...

!!!
`S THAT ALL? HERE Y' GO!

TRUST PIKE TO MAKE THE IMPOSSIBLE EASY. SOME HUNTERS WE ARE.
THE HUNT'S NOT OVER YET, CUTTER...

Y'KNOW... IF Y' WANT TO HUNT SOMETHING IMPRESSIVE, Y'OUGHT TO...
YES? GO ON! OUGHT TO WHAT??

ZZZZZZ
PTHEH...

PiiiiKE!
...OUGHT TO BRING BACK THAT HEAD THE HUMANS'VE BEEN LUGGING AROUND...

...BEARCLAW SAYS THEY CARRY A BIG OL' CARVED HEAD OF GODA... GRO... GOTARA TO GIVE 'EM LUCK ON HUNTS...

THAT'S A GREAT IDEA!
IT IS...?
HOLD ON... I KNOW WHAT YOU'RE THINKING... AND THE ANSWER IS NO!

A PEEK COULDN'T HURT US... AND HAVEN'T YOU WONDERED WHAT THIS "GOTARA" LOOKS LIKE?
WELLL...

AND IF WE GET THE CHANCE TO TAKE THE HEAD...
WE WON'T, BECAUSE IT WON'T, BECAUSE WE WON'T!

IT'D BE MUCH BETTER THAN A SILLY FLOWER...
WE LOOK, AND THAT'S ALL...
ZZZZZ

LATER...
WHAT A FEAST! THAT GOTARA HEAD MUST BE WORKING!
MAYBE, BUT THE SUMMER'S BEEN A GOOD ONE. THERE'S GAME ALL THROUGH THE WOODS.
DO YOU SEE IT...?
I'M NOT SURE... I HAVE NO IDEA WHAT THIS GOTARA LOOKS LIKE.
HOW ABOUT THAT UGLY THING?
UGH. NO WONDER THEY TAKE IT HUNTING. THE PREY SEES IT AND DROPS DEAD OF FRIGHT.
HEH HEH... LET'S GO GET IT...
CUTTER-- WE'VE STILL GOT OUR HUNT TO FINISH!
NOT YET. WE CAN WAIT. THE HUMANS WILL SLEEP SOON...
...AND THEN WE ADD TO OUR LIST...

MEANWHILE...
DO YOU REMEMBER HOW MAD WE GOT WHEN WE WERE SENT ON OUR FIRST DIGGER HUNT?
HEH HEH! MY BACK IS STILL SORE FROM ROOTING THROUGH ALL THOSE PAWFLOWERS...

I'VE YET TO FIND ONE...
I WOULD HAVE THOUGHT FOR CERTAIN THEY'D BE HERE...
...THEY'RE GONE...

INTO THE DREAMBERRIES ALREADY. TSK
WANT SOME? THEY'RE SO PLUMP...
PIKE, WHERE'S MY SON?

UMMM -- ON A DIGGER HUNT WITH WYSKISE?
I KNOW THAT-- HAVE YOU SEEN THEM?
NOT SINCE THEY WENT TO GET GOTATA'S HEAD...

WHAT? I NEVER SAID ANYTHING ABOUT...
OH NO! THEY DECIDED TO ADD TO THE LIST...

SHOULD WE GET THE OTHERS?
NOT YET, BROTHER. THIS WAS OUR IDEA -- LET'S HANDLE IT UNTIL WE NEED HELP...

YAWWWN WHAT ARE THEY DOING NOW?
STILL DANCING...

I NEVER KNEW THEY LIKED TO JUMP ABOUT SO MUCH.
IT COULD BE WORSE. THEY COULD BE SINGING.

IF BEARCLAW WERE HERE, HE'D JUST GO IN THERE AND GET THAT HEAD.
IF BEARCLAW WERE HERE, HE'D HAVE US TIED TO A TREE FOR EVEN BEING HERE.

YOU KNOW-- I'VE BEEN THINKING ABOUT HOW TO FIND A SLIVER OF MOONLIGHT...
REALLY?

"LET'S GO TO THE POND... AT GOODTREE'S GLEN..."

NOW, WHAT HAPPENS IF YOU TAKE UP A DOUBLE HANDFUL OF WATER.?

I SEE!! YOU'RE WISE ABOUT THE SKY INDEED!!
SO WITH THIS, AND THE GREEN DREAMBERRY, WE'VE GOT TWO OF THE THREE THINGS ON THE DIGGER HUNT LIST. ALL WE NEED IS THE FOUR-FINGERED PAW-FLOWER...

:GROAN: ARE YOU SAYING WE FORGET GOTARA'S HEAD AND GO SEARCHING AGAIN FOR IT?
WE WERE NEVER SUPPOSED TO RISK OUR LIVES ON THIS QUEST, YOU KNOW...

:SIGH: YOU'RE RIGHT. BESIDES, I DON'T THINK THOSE HUMANS ARE GOING TO STOP BEFORE SUNRISE...
BACK TO THE MEADOW, THEN...

...WE'VE GOT A "MAGIC" FLOWER TO FIND!

WHEW! HEH HEH...

THEY'RE SAFE. THEY'VE GOT NO "GOTARA'S HEAD"-- AND THERE ARE NO HUMANS AFTER THEM.
I WAS STARTING TO WONDER. CUTTER HAS MUCH OF HIS FATHER IN HIM.

LUCKILY, ENOUGH OF HIS MOTHER AS WELL.
DO YOU THINK THEY'LL SUCCEED WITH THE HUNT?
NO ELF HAS EVER BROUGHT BACK ALL THREE TREASURES... BUT IF I WERE THE WAGERING KIND, I'D PUT MY SKINS ON THOSE TWO.

MINE AS WELL, MY BROTHER-- MINE AS WELL.

MORNING...

SUN-HIGH...
GRUMBLE

DUSK...
SIGH THE DAY'S ALMOST GONE, SKYWISE...
WE'RE NOT GOING TO MAKE IT, I THINK.

I CAN'T GIVE UP! I WON'T!
IF ONLY THEY GREW ONE LESS...

...PETAL...
!!!

COME ON! I KNOW ANOTHER PLACE TO LOOK!!

THE MOONS ARE HIGH. HOW DID YOU TWO FARE ?

YOU CAN FIND ALMOST ANY-THING -- IF YOU KNOW WHERE TO GO TO...

...OR HOW TO SEE WHAT YOU'RE LOOKING FOR...

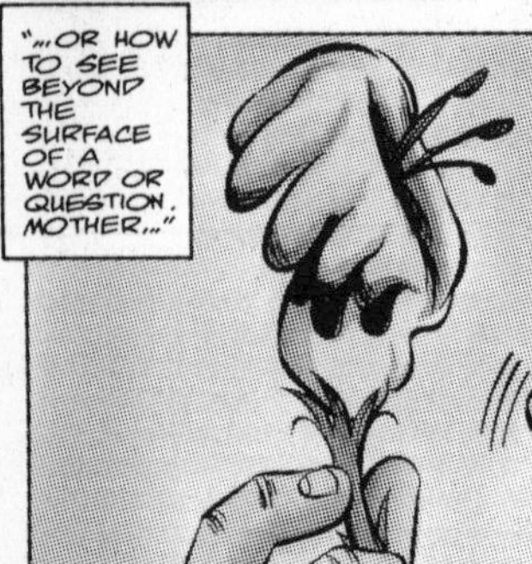
"...OR HOW TO SEE BEYOND THE SURFACE OF A WORD OR QUESTION, MOTHER..."

"...AND FIND WHAT'S REALLY ASKED FOR!"

HAH! A PERFECT HUNT! LET'S CELEBRATE! WITH SOME MORE DELICIOUS HONEY!
WHERE DID YOU SAY THAT STINGER HIVE WAS...?
THE END.

WHY DOES YOUR SMILE FADE SO SUDDENLY, SISTER?
SIGH...
WERE CUTTER A SHADE MORE HEADSTRONG --
-- HE'D HAVE GONE TO THE HUMANS' CAMP. HE DOESN'T REALLY KNOW, YET, WHAT THEY'RE CAPABLE OF!
"IT IS A PITY...BUT HE MUST LEARN TO TEMPER HIS FASCINATION WITH FAR GREATER CAUTION!"
M TA-TA-TUM TUM TA-TA-RUM TUM TU

WITH EACH NEW SEASON, THE WHITE-COLD HAS LESSENED.
<GOTARA! GOTARA! GOTARA!>
RUM TA TA TUM TUM
RUM TA TA TUM TUM
NOW THE TIME HAS COME.
THE BEAT OF THE WAR CHANT MATCHES THE BEAT OF THE SHAMAN'S HEART.
RUM TA TA TUM TUM
RUM TA TA TUM TUM
HIS YOUNG WARRIORS ARE FIRED WITH THE PASSION HE HAS NURTURED IN THEM.
<CHILDREN OF THE MASTER SPIRIT, ARE YOU READY TO DO HIS WILL?>
RUM TA TA TUM TUM
RUM TA TA TUM TUM

TABAK, THE YOUNG MEN'S NATURAL CAPTAIN, IS HOTLY READY.
<OH SHAMAN, WE WILL *CLEANSE* THE SACRED LAND AND *DESTROY* THE DEMONS!>
<YES! YES!>
<WE PLEDGE OUR LIVES TO IT!>
<WE SHALL NOT FAIL GOTARA!>
RUM TA TA TUM TUM
RUM TA TA TUM TUM
<AND, ONCE WE RECLAIM IT, WE SHALL *NEVER* BE DRIVEN FROM OUR LAND AGAIN!>
<BETTER TO SEE GOTARA *RAZE* IT...>
RUM TA TA TUM TUM
<...THAN LET THE FILTHY WOLF-DEMONS *DEFILE* IT ONE DAY LONGER!>
RUM TA TA TUM TUM
<TABAK, MY HEIR, WILL CARRY THE TALISMANS OF *VICTORY*.>
<THEY ARE IN HIS CARE, UNTIL WE HANG THEM ONCE MORE UPON THE PILLAR OF SACRIFICE.>
<AND I WILL BRING *NEW SKULLS* TO HONOR GOTARA!>
<*FOLLOW ME!* LET NO ONE STRAY OR FALL BEHIND!>
<NOW IS THE TIME TO *TAKE BACK* THE LAND GOTARA PROMISED TO *US ALONE!*>

LIFE HAS GONE ON AS USUAL IN THE HOLT, FULL OF HUNTING AND PLAY... FOR THE MOST PART FREE FROM CARE.

THE BRUISE HAS LONG SINCE FADED ON CUTTER'S CHEEK.

BUT ONE DAY AN *ODD SCENT,* ONE HE CANNOT QUITE PLACE, INTRODUCES A NOTE OF *DISQUIET...*
NNFF NNFF RRRRRR?
DON'T KNOW IT, FRIEND? SEEMS ALMOST... *FAMILIAR...* TO ME.
SKIDD-D-D-D!

STAY THERE, NIGHTRUNNER. I'LL TAKE A LOOK FIRST.

SNIFF SNIFF *STRONG.* IT'S *CLOSE BY...*

EH?! BY THE HIGH ONES!
GASP!!

THE STRANGE CREATURE - A SHE-CUB TOO YOUNG TO BE WANDERING ALONE - *STARES* AT HIM...
...WITHOUT FEAR.

GIGGLE
THIS LITTLE CUB DOESN'T FIT THE TALES I'VE HEARD OF *TROLLS.*
CLAP! CLAP! CLAP!
THAT MEANS IT MUST BE A-A *HUMAN!* BUT THERE'S NOTHING SCARY ABOUT IT.
LOOK AT THAT! *FIVE FINGERS* ON EACH HAND... JUST LIKE *SKYWISE* SAID!

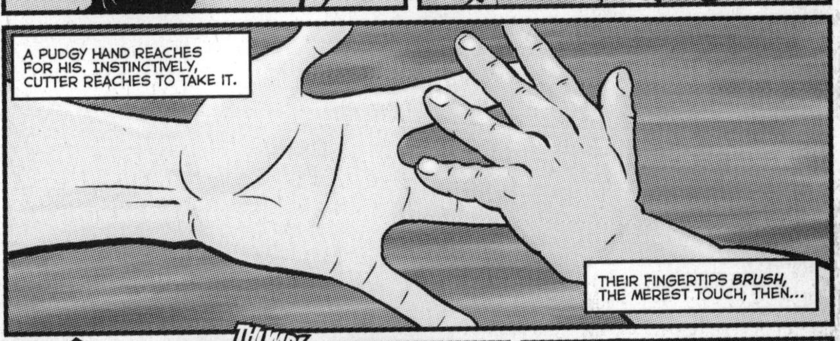
A PUDGY HAND REACHES FOR HIS. INSTINCTIVELY, CUTTER REACHES TO TAKE IT.
THEIR FINGERTIPS *BRUSH,* THE MEREST TOUCH, THEN...

<KLONI!? KLONNN-EEEEEE!>
THUMP!
KA-KRASSSH!
WHISSH!

NOT A SOUND, NIGHTRUNNER!
GRRRF!

<KLONI! *NEVER* WANDER OFF LIKE THAT, OR A *DEMON* MIGHT *EAT* YOU!>
CUTTER FINDS HIMSELF WISHING HE COULD *UNDERSTAND* THIS STRANGE, GUTTURAL TONGUE.

GUESS WHAT?! GUESS WHAT I SAW!
A HUMAN!!!

HIS TRIBEMATES GRIM FACES INSTANTLY DAMPEN YOUNG CUTTER'S ENTHUSIASM.
ALL THESE SEASONS OF PEACE... GONE.
BEARCLAW'S OFF CUTTING SPEAR-WOOD. I'LL SEND FOR HIM.

NO! THEY CAN'T BE BACK! *CHOKE* NOT AGAIN!
WHERE? HOW CLOSE? HOW MANY?
WAIT! BEARCLAW MUST BE HERE!

AS SOON AS BEARCLAW ARRIVES, A MUCH-SOBERED CUTTER RELATES WHAT HE SAW.
HIS FATHER'S TIGHT-LIPPED FEATURES... THE GRIEF AND FEAR AND RAGE HE FEELS FROM HIS TRIBE, LEAVE HIM BEWILDERED.

TREESTUMP, STRONGBOW, ONE-EYE, PIKE - COME WITH ME!
WE'LL SEE FOR OURSELVES!

I SAW THEM FIRST, FATHER! LET *ME* COME, TOO!
NOTHING DOING! STAY HERE!

SILENTLY JOYLEAF WAITS TO SEE IF HER SON WILL CHOOSE TO *FIGHT*...

...OR *GIVE IN*.
AS YOU WISH, MY CHIEF.
GOOD! I NEED YOU TO *PROTECT* THOSE THAT REMAIN HERE UNTIL WE RETURN!

SURPRISED AND PLEASED BEYOND MEASURE, CUTTER STANDS AS TALL AS HIS TWELVE TURNS OF THE SEASONS WILL ALLOW.
COUNT ON ME, FATHER!

THAT NIGHT, AFTER THE SCOUTING PARTY RETURNS, THERE IS A HEAVINESS IN THE HOLT...
IT'S TRUE. THEY'VE SET UP THEIR CAMP, SAME AS BEFORE.
THE OLD RULES MUST BE FOLLOWED. NO ONE GOES OUT IN DAYLIGHT.
NO ONE HUNTS OR GOES OFF ALONE - EVER!
A HUMAN CUB SAW CUTTER... BUT LETS HOPE THE TALL ONES DIDN'T BELIEVE ITS PRATTLE.
WE'RE GONE, AS FAR AS THEY KNOW.
LET'S KEEP IT THAT WAY... ALL OF YOU!
SO THE OLD, SAD DAYS OF HIDING AND KEEPING SILENT RETURN...
BUT SOME MONTHS LATER, REDMARK EARNS THE NEW NAME HIS CHIEF WILL GIVE HIM...
...REDLANCE!
RRROOOARRRRR!
UNH! GET OUT OF HIS WAY!
HIGH ONES! TOO LATE!
SCREEEECH!!
SNAPP!
AAAAGH!!
NIGHTFALL AND HER ORDINARILY MEEK LIFEMATE RUSH TO SUPPORT THEIR BADLY INJURED CHIEF...
WHAT OF THE CARCASS?
LATER! BEARCLAW NEEDS HEALER RAIN -- NOW!
SIGH HE NEEDS REST NOW... AS DO I. THE WOUNDS ARE DEEP.
THEY WILL TAKE MANY DAYS TO HEAL FULLY.
MANY DAYS... CURSE THE ROTTEN LUCK!

Courage, By Any Other Name...

SCRIPT- *WENDY & RICHARD PINI* PENCILS- *DEBBIE HAYES* INKS- *PAUL ABRAMS* LETTERS- *CLEM ROBINS*

BEARCLAW RULES THE WOLFRIDERS. IT IS HIS TIME. AND IT IS HIS KNOWLEDGE AND EXPERIENCE THAT NOW INSTRUCT YOUNG **NIGHTFALL** IN THE FINER POINTS OF BOW-HUNTING. **REDMARK**, NIGHTFALL'S LOVEMATE, WATCHES ADMIRINGLY AS SHE SIGHTS THE PREY.

BUT NIGHTFALL IS EVEN MORE AWARE OF BEARCLAW'S CRITICAL GAZE...

STEADY... KEEP THAT LEFT ARM STILL! NOW GENTLY... RELEASE!

AH! HE'S DOWN! AND THIS TIME YOU DIDN'T JERK YOUR ARM! WELL DONE!

SEE, REDMARK? I'VE IMPROVED! I--LOVEMATE! WHERE ARE YOU GOING?

HE HAS LITTLE TASTE FOR KILLING, BUT SOMETHING MORE THAN THAT TROUBLES HIM. IF ONLY I COULD HELP!

GO GET HIM. TELL HIM TO CHEER UP. I NEED BOTH OF YOU TO HELP TOTE THAT MEAT BACK TO THE HOLT.

A SHORT DISTANCE AWAY...
OLD TREE, I HEAR YOUR HEARTBEAT. YOU HAVE BLOOD AND BONES JUST AS I DO.

HOW GOOD IT WOULD BE TO FLOW WITH YOUR BLOOD, TO GROW WITH YOUR BONES--AS MY ANCESTORS COULD, TREE-SHAPERS...THEY KNEW THE JOY OF THE FULL USE OF THEIR MAGIC! THEY SHAPED THE HOLT AND THE FATHER TREE. THEY GAVE OUR TRIBE A HOME!

AND WHAT HAVE I GIVEN THE WOLFRIDERS? NOTHING!
IF THAT WERE TRUE, I WOULDN'T MISS YOU SO MUCH--EVEN WHEN YOU'RE GONE FOR JUST A MOMENT.

SOMETIMES YOU'RE MY ONLY COMFORT, NIGHTFALL. I FEEL SO... SO--
USELESS? BEARCLAW DOESN'T THINK SO! IN FACT, HE'LL HAVE BOTH OUR SKINS--

"--IF WE DON'T HURRY AND HELP HIM WITH THAT BUCK."
HMPH! HER AIM STILL NEEDS WORK ...IT'S NOT A CLEAN KILL.

AS BEARCLAW DELIVERS THE DEATH-STROKE--THE BUCK GIVES ONE LAST, CONVULSIVE KICK.

WHOOPF!

WHA--? OH, HAIRBALLS! NOT STRANGLEWEED!

STUPID...RROWR...CARELESS ...FRAZZ...GOT TO CUT MYSELF FREE BEFORE THE CUBS FIND OUT...!

LOOK!
(GIGGLE)

ONE WORD...EVEN SO MUCH AS A SMILE...

IT'S IMPOSSIBLE! THE HARDER I PULL, THE TIGHTER IT TWINES!
AND NEW TENDRILS MOVE IN TO REPLACE THE ONES I CUT! THIS WILL TAKE TIME, BEARCLAW!
A REAL TREE-SHAPER COULD UNTANGLE THIS MESS IN NO TIME.

REDMARK FLINCHES; HIS CHIEF'S TACTLESS JAB HAS HIT HOME.
HE'S RIGHT! WHY HAVE MY POWERS BEEN SO LONG IN COMING? WHY CAN'T I SUMMON THEM WHEN I NEED THEM?

HIGH ONES, PLEASE LET ME PROVE MYSELF...

UNNNHH... NOW! LET IT HAPPEN NOW!

GROAN! IT'S NO USE! I'M NO USE!

RUSTLE
SNARRL

GASP! A LONGTOOTH! HE SMELLS THE BUCK'S BLOOD!

KEEP CUTTING THE STRANGLEWEED! I'LL STOP HIS CHARGE!
NIGHTFALL!

SSSTHOKK
EEYOWRRR!
HURRY! HE'S WOUNDED --READY TO CHARGE AGAIN!
IN TIMMORN'S NAME BE CAREFUL!
RROOAR!
THIS SHOT HAS TO KILL!
WHUNG!

WHIZZZ!

NO! SHE MISSED! THE LONGTOOTH'S COMING!
YOU FOOL CUBS! RUN!
BUT REDMARK'S RESPONSE IS TO GRAB HIS SPEAR --

--AND BRACE IT AGAINST THE GROUND.
NO! I WON'T FAIL YOU AGAIN!

AAAARRR!

REDMARK! GET OUT OF HIS WAY! HIGH ONES! TOO LATE!

UNH!
SCREECH!

AAAA!
REDMARK! BEARCLAW!

SOB SOB

MY CHIEF! OH, HIGH ONES, I'M SORRY! IT SHOULD HAVE BEEN ME!

...IDIOT...!

THE OTHER WOLFRIDERS QUICKLY ARRIVE TO HELP REDMARK AND NIGHTFALL CARRY THEIR INJURED CHIEF TO THE FATHER TREE. NEARLY TWO GREATER MOONS WAX AND WANE WHILE BEARCLAW HEALS. BUT FINALLY...

MAYBE YOUR POWERS HAVEN'T SHOWN YET, CUB, BUT YOU STOOD YOUR GROUND AGAINST A PAIN-CRAZED CAT AND SAVED US BOTH! THAT'S THE RAREST KIND OF MAGIC. FROM NOW ON REDMARK, THE TRACKER, WILL BE CALLED ***REDLANCE,*** THE LONGTOOTH KILLER!

AND PERHAPS, SOMEDAY... REDLANCE, THE TREE SHAPER!

I FEAR YOUR FATHER WILL SOON BECOME BORED, LYING THERE IN OUR DEN.
WE MUST THINK OF WAYS TO KEEP HIM OCCUPIED... SO HE MAY HEAL.
I'LL FIND WAYS, MOTHER! LEAVE IT TO ME!

GOLDEN DAYS FOLLOW FOR CUTTER AS HE LISTENS TO BEARCLAW SPIN TALES OF THE CHIEFS BEFORE HIM.
HAH HAH! MY SIRE, OLD MANTRICKER, WAS A CUNNING ONE!
DID I TELL YOU OF THE TIME HE DROPPED A NEST OF YELLOW STINGERS ONTO A HUNTING PARTY THAT WAS AFTER 'IM?
THE BOND BETWEEN FATHER AND SON, SO HARD TO KEEP WHOLE, GROWS STRONGER THAN EVER.

BUT KEEPING BEARCLAW IN PLACE PROVES A CHALLENGING TASK.
WAIT! DON'T GET UP YET!
ER... THAT IS... I HAD AN IDEA! TEACH ME THE HUMAN TONGUE!

FORGETTING HIS BOOTS FOR A MOMENT, BEARCLAW SCOWLS AT THE THOUGHT...
UGLY, STUPID BABBLE. WHY WASTE YOUR TIME?
WELL... WHY DID YOU LEARN IT? ISN'T IT BETTER KNOWING WHAT AN ENEMY'S SAYING...?

...INSTEAD OF GUESSING - ACK!
HEH HEH! YOU'VE JOYLEAF'S WAY, HAVEN'T YOU? YOU THINK THINGS OUT AND ANSWER ME WITH REASON.
WELL, YOU'RE RIGHT. IF WE MUST DEAL WITH THE HUMANS AGAIN...

"...WE'D BETTER USE EVERY WEAPON WE HAVE!"
< FOR YOUR SPIRIT BAG, A LOCK OF YOUR HAIR... BONE FROM YOUR FIRST KILL... AND THE BLOODKIN HERB. >
< AND ESPECIALLY FOR YOU, *MY FAVORED ONE,* A CHIP OF BONE FROM A *DEMON SKULL...* >
< ...A TOKEN OF THE *KILLS* YOU WILL MAKE! >
< THE *HONOR* YOU DO ME IS TOO *GREAT,* OH MIGHTY SPIRIT MAN! >

JUST THEN...
<*SHAMAN!* SEE WHAT WE *FOUND!* >

< *DEMON WEAPONS!* I KNOW THEIR WORK! >
< AND, GOTARA WILLING, THE LONGTOOTH'S FANGS ARE SMEARED WITH *DEMON BLOOD!* >
< HOW CUNNINGLY THEY HAVE *HIDDEN* FROM US SINCE OUR RETURN! BUT NOW WE *KNOW...* >

< ...THEY ARE STILL *HERE!* >

"< LET THE *SACRED WAR BEGIN!!* >"
ONCE AGAIN LIFE BALANCES ON THE *BLADE'S EDGE.*

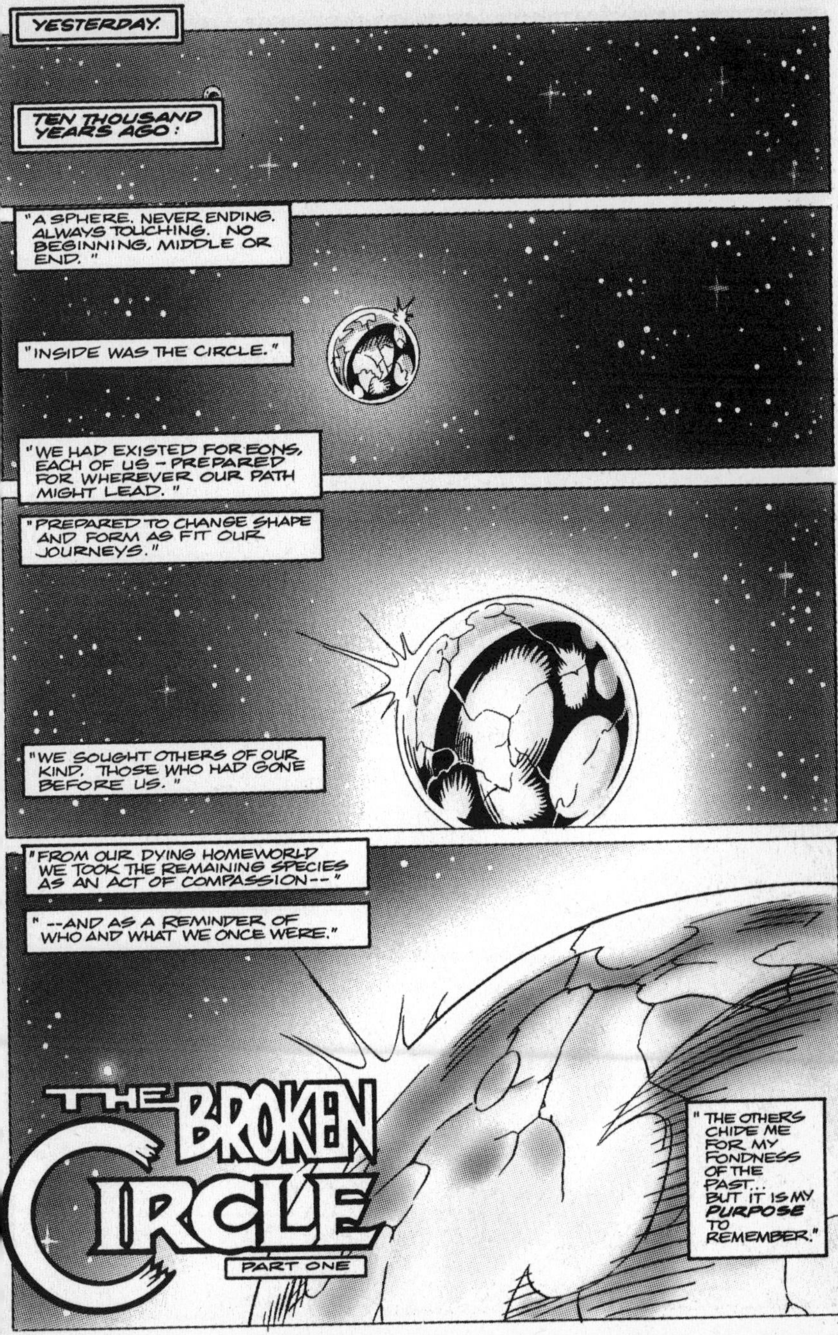

YESTERDAY.

TEN THOUSAND YEARS AGO:

"A SPHERE. NEVER ENDING. ALWAYS TOUCHING. NO BEGINNING, MIDDLE OR END."

"INSIDE WAS THE CIRCLE."

"WE HAD EXISTED FOR EONS, EACH OF US -- PREPARED FOR WHEREVER OUR PATH MIGHT LEAD."

"PREPARED TO CHANGE SHAPE AND FORM AS FIT OUR JOURNEYS."

"WE SOUGHT OTHERS OF OUR KIND. THOSE WHO HAD GONE BEFORE US."

"FROM OUR DYING HOMEWORLD WE TOOK THE REMAINING SPECIES AS AN ACT OF COMPASSION--"

"--AND AS A REMINDER OF WHO AND WHAT WE ONCE WERE."

THE BROKEN CIRCLE

PART ONE

"THE OTHERS CHIDE ME FOR MY FONDNESS OF THE PAST... BUT IT IS MY ***PURPOSE*** TO REMEMBER."

"AND NOW, ACCORDING TO ADYA, WE HAVE FOUND OUR LOST BROTHERS AT LAST."
IS IT NOT BEAUTIFUL, TIMMAIN?
FROM THE STARS, ALL WORLDS ARE EQUALLY BEAUTIFUL.
PERHAPS, HAKEN. BUT THIS ONE IS SPECIAL.
WE ALL SHARE YOUR JOY, ADYA.
SEFRA, WHAT IS THE MATTER?
THIS... ISN'T... RIGHT.
THIS PLANET **MUST** BE THE RIGHT ONE. I CAN FEEL THEIR ESSENCES...
NOT THE PLANET ...THE STARS.

THE STARS ARE WRONG.
KALIL! WHAT IS HAPPENING?
MOST STRANGE. WE'VE STOPPED MOVING.
"WE ARE CAUGHT BY THE WORLD'S PULL... AND I CAN'T ... SEEM TO... BREAK US FREE."
"WHAT IS THIS PLACE YOU HAVE BROUGHT US TO, ADYA? WHAT IS IT DOING TO ME?"

WE SHALL DISCOVER ANSWERS LATER. IF WE CAN'T GO UP, WE'LL GO DOWN. CAN YOU DO THIS, KALIL?
I... THINK SO. BUT I'LL NEED THE CIRCLE'S ASSISTANCE.
WE MUST CHANGE OURSELVES BEFORE REACHING THE PLANET'S SURFACE.
THE CREATURES BELOW MUST SEE US IN FORMS THEY ALREADY KNOW.
TIMMAIN-- WE ALL MUST JOIN TO CREATE THE CIRCLE.
I AM COMING.
"I CRAFTED A MESSENGER TO LET OTHERS OF OUR KIND KNOW WE WERE HERE."
"OUR STORY WAS SAFE... WAITING FOR THE RIGHT QUESTIONER."
"THE BEACON WOULD ORBIT THIS WORLD AS A THIRD MOON... UNTIL OUR DEPARTURE..."
"...WHENEVER THAT MIGHT BE."

THE WORLD OF TWO MOONS.
TEN THOUSAND YEARS LATER:
YOU SEE THAT BRIGHT STAR THERE... WHERE I'M POINTING?
IT'S YOURS.
MINE...?
I'M GIVING IT TO YOU.
FOXFUR'S STAR... I LIKE THE SOUND OF THAT.
I THOUGHT YOU MIGHT--
EH?
FOXFUR --LOOK AT THE SKY!
LATER, LOVEMATE...
ONE OF THE STARS ...IT'S FALLING!
NOT MY STAR, I HOPE.
NO, YOURS IS SAFE.
LOVELY.
I WONDER WHERE STARS GO WHEN THEY LAND?

BLAST YOUR THIEVING HIDE, ELF...
TAKE THE BLADE AND BE DONE WITH IT! USE IT TO SLICE YOUR OWN MISERABLE THROAT!
SOUR DREAM-BERRIES, PICK-NOSE?
AS SHARP AS EVER. YOU HAVEN'T LOST YOUR TOUCH AT THE FORGE.
TOO BAD YOU'RE NOT AS SKILLED AT THROWING THE STONES.
NO SKILL IN GAMES OF CHANCE, ELF-CHIEF. ONLY LUCK. YOURS HAS TO CHANGE SOMETIME TONIGHT.
HERE, PICKY! LET ME BLOW ON 'EM!
PUFF
PUFF
PUFF
HAH-HA! TOLD YOU! THREE TIMES THREE ON THE FIRST ROLL! BEAT THAT, BEARCLAW!

LUCK BOUGHT WITH TROLL'S BREATH IS NO LUCK AT ALL, PICKY.
THE SMELL ALONE IS ENOUGH TO DRIVE CHANCE BACK ON MY SIDE.
I'VE CLEANED YOU OUT-- YOU'LL HAVE TO BET YOUR TROLL WENCH NEXT!
HA! THREE TIMES THREE BACK AT YOU! WE'LL BOTH HAVE TO ROLL-- TO ROLL AGAIN--
WHAT'S THE MATTER, ELF? PRESSURE GETTING TO YOU?
PERHAPS ONE DRINK TOO MANY!
OF THIS - WEAK TROLL WINE? YOU WISH! EARBUG I BELIEVE - IT'S YOUR--
-- TURNNN --

BY THE HIGH ONES... SUCH PAIN...
BEARCLAW!
MOTHER?
GCGKK--! MY HEAD!
SKYWISE! WHAT'S WRONG?
...THE CIRCLE ...NINE OF US TO CREATE ...THE CIRCLE...

MOTHER? DID YOU HIT YOUR HEAD?
NO, CUB. BUT IT STILL ACHES FOR SOME REASON.
MY HEAD HURTS TOO! LIKE A BUG'S FLYING AROUND INSIDE AND I CAN'T SHAKE IT OUT.
REALLY? A BUZZING SOUND IS WHAT I HEAR AS WELL...
I SAW YOUR FATHER BEFORE I FELL. THE TWO MUST BE RELATED.
WE MUST RIDE TO THE HIDDEN ENTRANCE OF --
"-- THE CAVERN OF THE TROLLS."
OPEN UP IN THERE! I SEEK BEARCLAW, CHIEF OF THE WOLFRIDERS!
CLANG! KATANG
ENOUGH WITH YOUR POUNDING ELF! YOU WANT BEARCLAW?
YOU CAN HAVE HIM!
PICKNOSE! IF YOU'VE HARMED MY LIFEMATE, I'LL--!

YOU'LL WHAT ?! STUPID TREE WOLF! WHY THREATEN ME IF YOUR MANGY MATE CAN'T HOLD HIS DRINK!?
YOU TELL BEARCLAW-- SINCE HE'S THE ONE WHO PASSED OUT, HIS WINNINGS ARE FORFEIT!
GIVE THAT BACK!
HEE-HEE-HEE!
SLAM
UNNNN--!! MY HEAD'S KILLING ME!
GET DRUNK AND YOU SUFFER THE CONSE-QUENCES.
I'VE TAKEN FAR MORE THAN THIS AND KEPT MY FEET BENEATH ME!
AND THEN THIS HIVE OF INSECTS BUZZING AROUND IN MY SKULL...!
BUZZING?!

LET ME FREE !!
ALL THE TRIBE IS AFFECTED, MY CHIEF--
-- SOME WORSE THAN OTHERS.
I'VE GOT TO FIND THEM...
...BEFORE IT'S TOO LATE!
FIND WHO? WHAT'S CAUSING THIS, HEALER?
I... DO NOT KNOW.
IT'S NOT A SICKNESS OF THE BODY. THE PAIN COMES FROM THE MIND.
IT TOOK THREE OF US TO CATCH ONE-EYE. HE WAS RACING AROUND LIKE HE WAS CRAZED WITH THE FOAMING SICKNESS.
AND THEN THERE'S SKY-WISE.
FOXFUR BROUGHT HIM TO ME, BUT I CAN'T WAKE HIM UP.
I'M NOT SURE I WANT TO. I THINK THE SLEEP MIGHT BE PART OF A HEALING PROCESS.
GIVE ME A FOE I CAN FACE AND I'LL TAKE HIM ON-- GLADLY! BUT THIS REEKS OF MAGIC!
OLD, BAD MAGIC...THIS IS BEYOND ME.
EVERYONE I'VE SPOKEN TO IS REST-LESS, READY TO GO FORWARD... BUT WHERE OR WHY, I CAN'T ANSWER.
HEALER!
WE WERE TALKING... AND SHE SUDDENLY KEELED OVER.

SHE'S SLEEPING... JUST LIKE SKYWISE.
CAN'T YOU HELP HER, RAIN?
NO.
DEWSHINE!
EASY, SCOUTER. SHE'S SLEEPING-- THAT'S ALL.
DEW-SHINE? CAN YOU HEAR ME?
OH, PLEASE SAY SOME-THING--!
COME, LET THEM REST.
...CIRCLE...
CIRCLE? WHAT ARE YOU DREAMING, BROTHER?

...THE CIRCLE...
"OTHERS, SUCH AS MYSELF, STAYED BEHIND..."
"UNTIL OUR SUN BEGAN TO DIE... AND THEN WE KNEW WE MUST GO FORWARD."
"WE TOOK THE FLITRINS AND THE BURROWERS WITH US. THEY WERE MISCHIEVOUS..."
"THE OTHERS TOLD ME TO LEAVE THEM, BUT I INSISTED."
"ALL LIFE IS PRECIOUS, AND WORTH PRESERVING."

"OUR WORLD WAS FULL... AND HAD SUFFERED FROM OUR YOUTHFUL INDISCRETIONS."
"SOME LEFT TO EASE THE PRESS OF SO MANY BODIES."
"AND WHEN WE FOUND OTHERS, WE MOLDED OUR VERY FLESH -- AND OUR TRANSPORT -- TO REFLECT WHAT THEIR MINDS COULD ACCEPT."
"BUT THEN ... THE CIRCLE WAS BROKEN--"
"--WAS BROKEN--"
"--BROKEN."
NO! NOT YET! NOT YET!
WE CREATED THE CIRCLE, EACH OF US GIVING OUR OWN TALENT OVER TO A STRONGER WHOLE."

IF SOMETHING CALLS ME OUT FOR A FIGHT, I TAKE IT ON! SIMPLE AS THAT.
THIS COULD BE A TRAP...
WHAT IF IT IS? IF SO, LET'S MEET IT AND TURN IT!
ANYTHING TO GET THIS CURSED BUZZING OUT OF MY BRAIN.
THE SOUND IS LIKE A WHISPER IN THE MIND--
NOT FOR ME--
--I HEAR SINGING.
YOU'RE AWAKE? GOOD!
WHAT'S THIS SINGING SOUND LIKE?
UM, DID YOU EVER HAVE A TUNE ON THE TIP OF YOUR TONGUE...
BUT COULDN'T RECALL THE WORDS?

WHAT KIND OF AN ANSWER IS THAT?
THE BEST I HAVE. WHAT'S ECHOING IN MY HEAD FEELS LIKE AN INVITATION -- I CAN'T SAY IT IN WORDS.
ENOUGH WITH WORDS, THEN -- I SAY LET OUR ACTIONS SPEAK!
WAITING IS USELESS... IF SOMETHING CALLS US WE SHOULD SEEK IT OUT.
WE'LL TRAVEL BY NIGHT -- A SMALL PARTY TO DIG OUT WHAT'S DOING THIS --
-- AND DRIVING SOME OF OUR KIN TO MADNESS.
SKYWISE, IS DEWSHINE-- ?
STILL SLEEPING, SCOUTER. SHE'LL WAKE UP SOON -- I KNOW IT.
I'M CURIOUS TO KNOW IF HER DREAMS WERE LIKE MINE... WHAT LITTLE I CAN REMEMBER OF THEM.

WE LEAVE NOW. THIS MIGHT STOP, IT MIGHT NOT-- BUT WHATEVER IT IS, IT HAS HURT THE TRIBE.
FIVE ONLY WILL GO. I CHOOSE--
"--SCOUTER, FOR HIS KEEN EYES--"
"--NIGHTFALL, FOR HER AIM--"
"--TREESTUMP, FOR HIS LOVE OF A GOOD FIGHT--"
"--AND JOYLEAF, FOR HER JUDGMENT."
THE REST OF YOU WAIT HERE. WE WILL RETURN AS SOON AS WE CAN.
TELL DEWSHINE WHEN SHE AWAKENS I'LL BE BACK FOR HER.

CHIEFTESS... I WANT TO GO WITH YOU.
NO, SKYWISE, YOU MUST REMAIN HERE.
I KNOW YOU SEE YOUR OWN VISION OF WHAT HAS ENTERED THE HOLT, BUT ALL I FEEL IS EVIL.
IF IT'S AS DARK AS I SENSE, YOU ARE NOT YET READY TO FACE SUCH A FOE.
BUT-- BUT I CAN FEEL IT CALLING ME...
ALL THE MORE REASON TO STAY.
WATCH OVER MY SON, SKYWISE.
AW, PUCKERNUTS! I'M TIRED OF BEING TREATED LIKE A CUB!
YOU'LL GET USED TO IT...
NOT THIS TIME! I CAN MAKE A CHOICE TOO!
?
I'M FOLLOWING THEM --ARE YOU WITH ME?
BEARCLAW WILL HAVE BOTH OUR HEADS.
ONLY IF HE CATCHES US TO CHOP THEM OFF. DON'T WORRY-- WE'LL KEEP OUR DISTANCE.
WE'D BETTER.

TIME FOR ⁑YAWN⁑ SLEEP. I'D HATE TO TRIP OVER A SNOOZING WOLFRIDER IN MY PATH.
SOUNDS GOOD. LET'S FIND ANOTHER TREE.
OWWOOOOOOWWWW
WHA--?
BLACKFELL!
BUT WHERE'S BEARCLAW-- AND THE OTHERS?
FOR SOME REASON, THEY WENT AHEAD ON FOOT FROM HERE. I CAN SEE THEIR TRACKS.
I THINK I KNOW WHY.

THE WOLVES WOULDN'T GO ANY FURTHER.
NOW NIGHTRUNNER AND STARJUMPER ARE SPOOKED, TOO!
WHAT IS HAPPENING, WOLF-FRIEND? WHY DO YOU HESITATE?
...STAY ...NO GO... STAY...
THAT'S THAT.
LOOKS LIKE WE'RE ON OUR OWN THE REST OF THE WAY.
WE MUST BE GETTING CLOSE.
I SAY WE HOLD OFF ON THAT NAP.

STILL... ELVES SHOULD NEVER GO WHERE WOLVES FEAR TO TREAD.
TRY SENDING --I'M BEYOND CARING IF WE GET CAUGHT OR NOT.

ANYTHING?
NOTHING.
ME NEITHER.
MAYBE WE SHOULD GO BACK TO THE HOLT FOR HELP..
CUTTER! IT'S BACK! THE SINGING ...LOUDER NOW!

AK! SO'S THE BUZZING. BUT I'M GOING TO IGNORE IT.
I SAY WE FIND BEARCLAW THE HARD WAY-- WE TRACK HIM. WE CAN CHASE SINGING BUGS LATER.

I'D FORGOTTEN HOW HOT THE SUN COULD BE.
SHHH! DO YOU HEAR ANYTHING?
NO. THE WOODS ARE QUIET.
TOO QUIET. NO WIND. NO BIRDS.
COME ON, THE TRAIL LEADS THIS WAY.
FATHER? MOTHER? ANSWER ME, PLEASE!
GASP CUTTER-- LOOK!

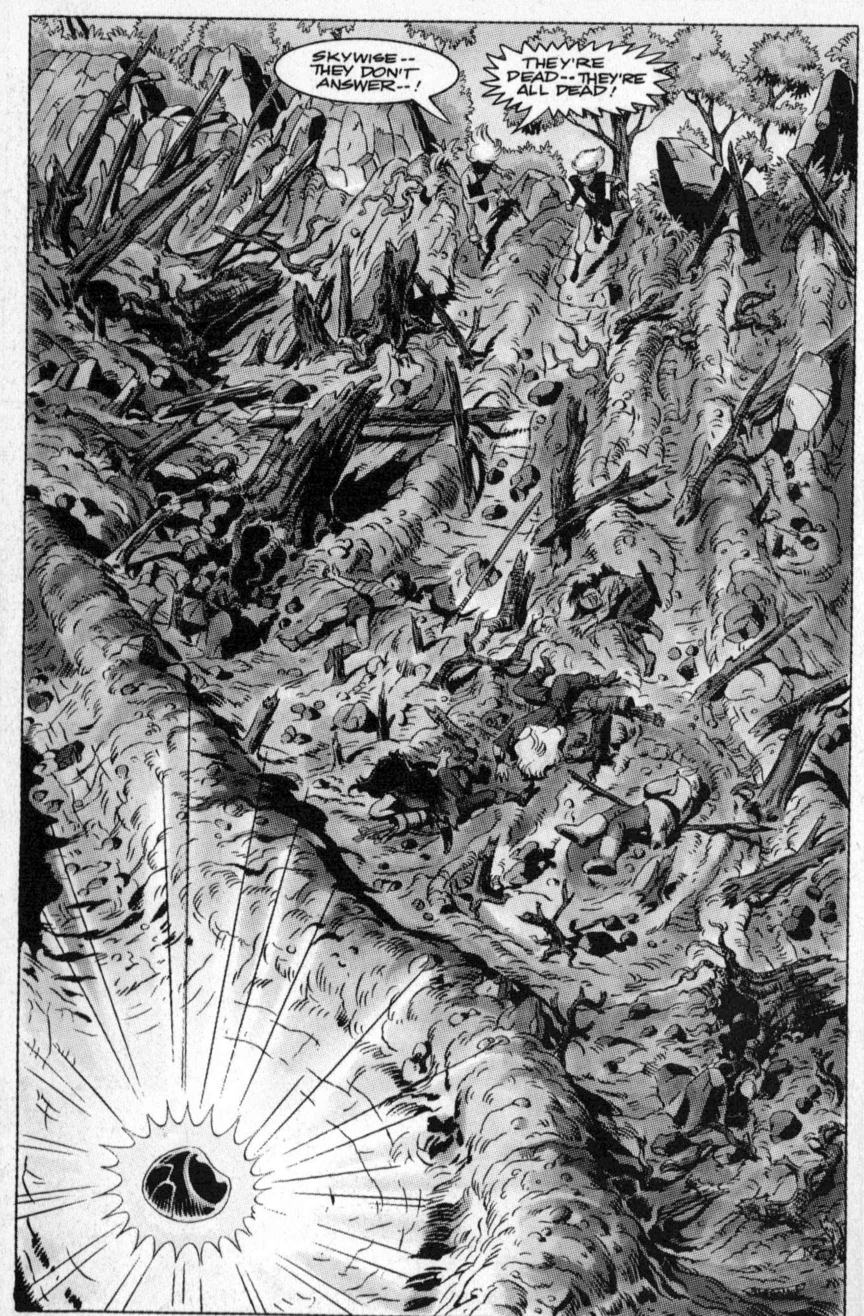
SKYWISE--
THEY DON'T
ANSWER--!
THEY'RE
DEAD--THEY'RE
ALL DEAD!

SLEEPING --JUST LIKE THE OTHERS.
THE BROKEN CIRCLE - PART TWO

LIKE WHAT HAPPENED TO YOU AND DEWSHINE BACK AT THE FATHER TREE.
AND I WOKE UP. THEY WILL TOO.
DON'T UNH WORRY.
THE LIGHT COMING FROM THAT HOLE MUST BE CAUSING ALL THIS.
LET'S SEE IF WE CAN GET A CLOSER LOOK--
BEFORE THIS... BUZZING IN MY HEAD... CAUSES ME TO--

Oohhhh--
WHOOAA!
YOU WERE SAYING?
YOU WON'T NEED THIS NOW...
SLEEP WELL, MY BROTHER.
I'LL SEE - FOR BOTH OF US - WHAT'S BEEN CALLING TO ME.

???

OHHHH, PUCKERNUTS...

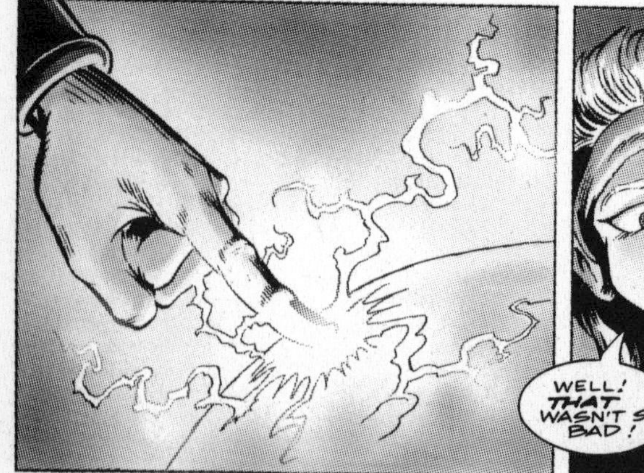

WELL! THAT WASN'T SO BAD!

ALLLL RIIIGHHTTT...

NOW, LET'S TAKE A CLOSER
UMPH
LOOK.

HUHHHHNNNN...! COME ON...

TIMMORN'S BLOOD! CAN THIS BE...?

HAS A STAR FALLEN DOWN FROM THE HEAVENS?
A STAR-- THAT SINGS IN A VOICE ONLY I CAN HEAR?

STILL NO CHANGE, CUB. SOON AS THEY AWAKEN, I'LL TELL YOU.
TRY AND GET SOME REST... THESE RECENT DAYS HAVE EXHAUSTED ALL OF US.
HE'S WORRIED-EVERYONE WHO'S LEFT IS.
I'VE NEVER SEEN ANYTHING LIKE THIS.
POOR SCOUTER...
OH!
WHOA--!
DEWSHINE! YOU'RE AWAKE!
RAIN... I HAD THE MOST INCREDIBLE DREAM.

"I WAS FLYING HIGH IN THE SKY, --"
"--LIKE A BIRD WITHOUT WINGS."
"I COULD LOOK DOWN AND SEE THE TREES."
"SUDDENLY I WAS CHANGING INTO SOMETHING --MORE THAN WOLFRIDER."
"THERE WAS MUSIC... I COULD HEAR MANY VOICES SINGING TOGETHER."
"BUT I WASN'T FRIGHTENED. I KNEW I HAD BEEN CHOSEN TO SING WITH THEM."
BUT-- I CAN'T REMEMBER THE WORDS NOW...

HM. FEELS SOFT HERE -- LIKE AN OLD BRUISED TUNKBERRY.
MUST HAVE HAPPENED WHEN YOU HIT THE GROUND.
AND HIT HARD, TOO.
GGG. STICKY HERE... BROKEN?
BUT WHATEVER, IT HASN'T STOPPED THE MUSIC I'M HEARING -- HMP. THAT'S FUNNY...
GASP

HEY! LET GO!

TIMMORN'S BLOOD!

WELL! YOU'RE FULL OF TRICKS!

BUT YOU'RE NOT WITHOUT YOUR LIMITS. FLOATING SURE TOOK THE WIND OUT OF YOU.

COULD THIS BE A PIECE OF OLD MAGIC-- LEFT BEHIND BY...
OW!
I-I DON'T UNDERSTAND YOUR WORDS.
WHAT ARE YOU SAYING?

BY THE HIGH ONES--!

WHA-?! A SPIRIT?
I AM SKYWISE.
WHO ARE YOU?

WAIT! DON'T GO!!
YOU CAN'T GO--
--not yet.
OOOWWWWOOOOO
OOOWWWWOOOO
OOOWWWOOOOOWWWOO
OOOOOOWO
THE PACK CANNOT KNOW THE SOURCE OF THE HOWL-- BUT THEY KNOW ITS ANGUISHED CONTENT, AND MUST SHARE...

THAT CAN'T BE ALL... IT CAN'T END LIKE THIS!
I WON'T LET IT BE OVER!
THEY HAVEN'T COME OUT OF THEIR SLEEP.
AND I STILL HEAR THE MUSIC.
THIS ISN'T FINISHED.
HOWEVER ...WHATEVER I DID...
I HAVE TO TRY AGAIN...
I...

FOR AEONS IT CIRCLED THE LARGER BODY, CARRYING ITS TIMELESS SECRETS.
UNTIL SIMPLE COSMIC CHANCE TOOK IT FROM ITS ENDLESS ORBIT...
...AND GAVE IT IN FIERY BIRTH TO THE WORLD OF TWO MOONS...
...WHERE IT COULD SING ITS MULTI-HUED SYMPHONY...

...DIRECTLY INTO THE DAZZLED MIND OF ONE SMALL ELF...
T-too much! It hurts!
STOP THE MUSIC...

STOP IT!

"STOPPPPPP...."

...ARE ...YOU THERE?

OH... OHHHHH.

NO DREAMBERRY VISION WAS EVER LIKE THAT... WHAT DID I ***SEE***??

I'VE GOT TO...

BUT THEN...
...FAHR...

...FAHR...
NEVER THOUGHT... ANYTHING COULD HURT SO MUCH...
IT KNOWS MY SOUL NAME! IT KNOWS!
TOO... BRIGHT... TOO LOUD...
GOT... TO STOP IT...
WHOOOF
GOT...TO...
HIGH ONES... HELP... ME...

UHH!
HELP... ME...
:sob:
I'm sorry...

UHHHH! TIMMORN'S HAIRBALLS...!
OHHH!
DEWSHINE! WHERE...?

SKYWISE?

WHAT HAPPENED HERE?

IT WAS SO BEAUTIFUL, BEARCLAW.

WE COULDN'T HEAR--
--NONE OF US.
I THOUGHT I COULD, BUT I WASN'T READY. I WASN'T STRONG ENOUGH.
IT WAS SINGING...

EIGHT AND FOUR DAYS LATER...

ARE YOU...?

IT CAME FROM UP THERE... I **KNOW** IT.
WHAT?

THE GLOWING BALL. IT CAME FROM... WHERE THE STARS ARE.
ERRRRR! I'D ALMOST FORGOTTEN THAT THING.

BUT YOU-- ONCE YOU SET YOUR MIND ON SOMETHING, THAT'S IT.
THE SON OF BEARCLAW IS CALLING **ME** STUBBORN?

YOU MAKE TOO MUCH OF THE STARS, BROTHER. THEY'RE JUST LITTLE LIGHTS.
HMMM?

CUTTER,
EVERYTHING COMES FROM THE STARS!
I-- KNOW IT...
DO THEY FEED AND WARM US?
DO THEY PROTECT US FROM HARM?
NO.

I'D RATHER FIND OUT MORE ABOUT THE LANDS THAT SURROUND THE HOLT BEFORE MY HEAD GOES FLYING OUT IN THE STARS.

SOMEDAY... I'LL SEE THEM UP CLOSE.
WELLLL...

I'LL MEET YOU BACK AT THE HOLT.

SOMEDAY...
THE END

TWO AND SOME TURNS OF THE SEASONS HAVE PASSED. TO BEARCLAW, WITH TWELVE HUNDRED YEARS BEHIND HIM, TWO ARE BARELY A BLINK...
...AND HIS ANGER REMAINS FRESH.
CARRION ROT AND BAT DUNG! FIRST, THE HUMANS COME BACK...
...THEN THIS! CURSE MY LUCK!
KLAK-TA-KLAK!
HE TRIES TO BURY HIS ANGER DEEP UNDERGROUND... TO DULL THE EDGE OF IT WITH THE DUBIOUS BLISS OF DREAMBERRY WINE...

...WINE WHICH CRAFTY KING GREYMUNG IS MORE THAN WILLING TO PROVIDE.
HAND IT OVER! IT'S A WAGER FAIRLY WON, WOLFRIDER.
SAVE YOUR SCOWLS FOR THE FIVE-FINGERS.
PHAUGH! TAKE IT, THEN!
CHISELS AND TONGS! I'VE BEEN TRYING TO WIN THIS BACK SINCE THE WATER-PILLARS 'ROUND MY THRONE WERE NUBS!
DON'T GROW FOND OF THE FEEL OF IT, TROLL-KING.
I'M NOT LEAVING 'TIL IT'S MINE AGAIN.
OH, HO, A CHALLENGE, IS IT? NOT BAD... FOR AN ELF!
YOU SHOULD'VE BEEN BORN A TROLL, PINK-SKIN, YOU SHOULD'VE BEEN BORN A TROLL!!
swipe!
A TOAST... *HIC* TO BEARCLAW, WICKEDEST CHIEFTAIN OF ELVES...
GLURRRG!
...TERROR OF THE HUMANS!!

ABOVE GROUND, BROWNBERRY AND FOXFUR GO ABOUT GATHERING... LISTENING NERVOUSLY TO EVERY SOUND...
SEE? TOLD YOU THERE'D BE MORE NESTS HERE!
SOMETHING DOESN'T FEEL RIGHT. IT'S TOO QUIET.
WE HAVE PLENTY, NOW. LET'S TAIL IT!
KRRKKKK!
THE SOUND IS SHARP, MADE BY A HEAVY FOOT.
IN THE ELVES' MEMORY, THE RECENT-ENOUGH DEATHS OF SHALE, EYES-HIGH AND CRESCENT STILL BURN...
AND WITH THEM THE FEAR - WILL THEY BE NEXT?
FOXFUR! SMELL THEM?!
-- YES, THEY'RE CLOSE!

ULP
NO ... THEY'RE HERE!
<KEEP YOUR SPEARS STEADY! GOTARA WILL CURSE US FOREVER IF WE LOSE THIS SACRIFICE!>
<WE HAVE THEM! WE HAVE THE DEMONS! HAIII! HAIII!>
<WE KILL THEM NOW, YES, TABAK?>
<YES, WE WILL TAKE NO CHANCES! KILL THEM!>
BROWNBERRY... THE BIG, BAD-SMELLING ONE... CAN YOU UNDERSTAND WHAT HE SAYS?
NO NEED! HIS MEANING IS CLEAR ENOUGH!
HNNH!
KTAK!!
CLUMSY TRY, TALL ONE!
OUR WOLVES ARE CLOSE BY. WE MUST TRY A WOLF-SEND!
I AM... ! NNNGH!

AS FOXFUR AND BROWNBERRY DESPERATELY PARRY THE HUMANS' SPEARS...
AARROOOOOOOO
<LISTEN! EVIL WOLVES COME TO HELP THE DEMONS!>
THE HOWLS GIVE THE ELF MAIDENS STRENGTH TO FIGHT ON.
<WE WILL KILL THEM, TOO, FOR THE GLORY OF GOTARA!>
FOXFUR, WE MUST GET PAST THE HUMANS, LEST THEY HARM OUR WOLF-FRIENDS!
FOLLOW ME!
SPLOOTCH!
SPUTCH!
<*BLEFFFF!*>
AWIP!
OGH! *COUGH* *COUGH*
COUGH HUKK!
NOOOOOOO!!
<STOP THEM!!!>

<KILL! KILL!>
RUN, RATTLE-RIBS!
PANT PANT PANT
TABAK'S FURY IS GREAT AS THE PREY ELUDES HIM...
WHISSHH!
<GHAAAAARRRR!!!>
SSHIKK!
YAAAAHHH!

HSSS! BUT WE WERE NOWHERE NEAR THE HUMAN CAMP...!
THAT'S PLAIN ENOUGH, SHE-CUB...
WHY WOULD THEY COME IN SO FAR FROM THEIR USUAL TERRITORY?
...THEY'RE HUNTING SOMETHING OTHER THAN THEIR USUAL GAME.
WE SHOULD STRIKE FIRST... RAID 'EM AND FINISH 'EM OFF!
THEY'RE MEAT TO BE WASTED!
SUCKING BOGS! WHERE IS BEARCLAW?
HE KEEPS GOING AWAY. IT'S BEEN DAYS.
SIGH HE'S STILL DOING "BUSINESS" WITH THE TROLLS, I'M AFRAID.
YOU CAN ACT AS CHIEF, JOYLEAF. TELL US WHAT TO DO!
REMAIN CLOSE TO THE HOLT. DO NOTHING UNTIL BEARCLAW RETURNS.
CUTTER FEELS THE DEEP UNHAPPINESS OF THE TRIBE.
IF HIS FATHER CANNOT BE HERE TO HELP THEM, PERHAPS HIS SON CAN.

WHY NOT *TALK* TO THE HUMANS? IF WE COULD WORK OUT A PEACE--
--PEACE! HAHAH! *GOOD ONE,* CUTTER-CUB!

THERE'S *NO* TALKING TO 'EM. THEY ONLY UNDERSTAND *BLOOD!*
BUT... HAS ANYONE *TRIED?*

YOU'RE TOO YOUNG TO UNDERSTAND, SON OF BEARCLAW.
BUT HE'S BEEN TEACHING ME THEIR *TONGUE!* WHAT IF WE--
--CUTTER! THAT'S *ENOUGH!*

HOPING TO CHANNEL HIS ADOLESCENT ENERGIES, JOYLEAF GUIDES HER SON AND HIS FRIEND *NIGHTFALL* TO THE EDGE OF THE HOLT.
I WANT YOU BOTH TO KEEP WATCH HERE. SEND TO ME THE MOMENT YOU SEE BEARCLAW RETURNING.

NOT FOOLED FOR A MOMENT, CUTTER SULLENLY NODS.

THEY WOULDN'T *LISTEN.* I'M *TIRED* OF BEING TOLD I'M TOO YOUNG!
DO YOU REALLY THINK YOU CAN TALK TO *HUMANS?*
MAYBE I *AM* CRAZY, BUT **SOMEONE** HAS TO TRY!

YOU BELIEVE IN ME, DON'T YOU, NIGHTFALL?

I BELIEVE IN YOU. AND I'LL FOLLOW WHEREVER YOU LEAD.

GOOD! BUT NOT NOW! STAY AND KEEP WATCH.

I'LL BE BACK WHEN I'VE *MADE PEACE.*

GASP!

FOR LONG, AGONIZING MOMENTS, NIGHTFALL STRUGGLES WITH INDECISION.

HE IS HER DEAREST FRIEND. THE LAST THING SHE'D WISH IS TO BETRAY HIS TRUST...

BUT, IN THE END, ***FEAR*** FOR CUTTER'S LIFE OVERRIDES ALL.

JOYLEAF...!!

AT THE SAME TIME, IN THE TROLLS' DEN...
AH HAH!
RATTLE
RATTLE
PLOP!
PLOP!
ISH MINE AGIN.' *HIC!* LOOKEE... WUNNITBACK, Y'OLD STINKWIND BAG!
WOOOOOMPH!!
SNRRRRZZZZLL
MOAN HOW LONG ... I BEEN HERE, OL' MAGGOTY? GOTTA GET BACK.
YOU CAN'T LEAVE YET, BROWNBEARD. NOT WITHOUT SAMPLING MY LATEST BATCH OF BREW. *CACKLE*
EH? WELL... ONE MORE... THASH IT.
GLUGGLGGG
UH...

AND, LIKE A MIGHTY OAK FELLED BY A STORM WIND...
ka-FLOPP!

HENH HENH HENH
ZZZNAAAAAH...
ZZZZZZRRRRGLE...

<I FAILED YOU, MY SHAMAN. BIND ME TO THE PILLAR OF SACRIFICE! STRIP MY SKULL OF FLESH!>
<NO, TABAK. ONE DOES NOT SPEND MANY MOONS CHIPPING OUT A FINE, BLACKSTONE BLADE...>
<ONLY TO SNAP IT IN TWO AND CAST IT ASIDE!>

<HOY, OLD ONE! COME OUT! ME YOU TO SPEAK!>
GASP! <A DEMON VOICE... CALLING TO ME!>

<LOOK! IT'S ALONE!>
<WAIT! THEY USED A TRICK SUCH AS THIS TO KILL MY TEACHER!>

<YOU NO KILL US... US NO KILL YOU!>
<LIVE FOREST ONE PEOPLE! SHARE, SAYS CUTTER, SON OF CHIEF!>
THE SHAMAN'S FACE LIGHTS UP WITH DREAMS OF VENGENCE ...
<SON OF THE DEMON-CHIEF! THE PERFECT SACRIFICE!>
OH, PUCKERNUTS!!
<BRING HIM ALIVE!>
BOKK!
OOWWW!
<CATCH THE DEMON!>
TOO LATE, STRONGBOW'S ADMONITION RETURNS TO HAUNT HIM...
"...THERE'S NO TALKING TO 'EM THEY ONLY UNDERSTAND BLOOD!"
POUNDING RED PAIN DRAGS HIM DOWN INTO DARKNESS AS...

A-RASSHH!!
AAYOOOOOAAAAH!!
GRRROWLLL!
EEEEYAAAAH!
RRRRROOWWWRRR!
SNAAARLL!
STRONGBOW, WE'LL COVER YOU! SAVE CUTTER!
AAIIEEEE!
THE HUMANS INSTINCTIVELY DRAW BACK FROM THE ELF YOUTH'S BATTERED BODY, AND...
WOULD'VE GLADLY SKEWERED YOU ALL, FILTH...!
...BUT MY CHIEF'S SON COMES FIRST!
SWOOP!
BACK TO THE HOLT! GO!
POIMMG!
WHILE THE REST OBEY, A LIVID JOYLEAF FIRES A PARTING ARROW AT THE SHAMAN.
<HA HA HA! GOTARA PROTECTS ME FROM YOUR WEAPONS, DEMON!>
SSSNIKT!
<THAT YOUNG ONE SHALL DIE! AND SOON I WILL DESTROY YOU ALL!>

DRAWING ON EVERY PARTICLE OF HIS GIFT, RAIN TAXES HIS ABILITY TO HEAL AS NEVER BEFORE.
IN THE HIGH ONES' NAME, SAVE HIM... YOU MUST!
THE HEALER HAS LOST OTHER SUCH BATTLES... AND BORNE THE GUILT.
BUT THIS ONE HE CANNOT LOSE.
BEARCLAW! YOU MUST COME...! COME!!
BEARCLAW!
BEARCLAW, ANSWER ME! I NEED YOU!
BEARCLAW!
THE ELFIN CHIEF STIRS UNEASILY AS THE SENDING PASSES THROUGH HIS DREAMBERRY-BESOTTED MIND.
HE DREAMS OF BLOOD, OF DANGER, OF CRUEL LOSS.
BUT HE DOES NOT WAKE.

ARCLAW REMAINS IN THE
ON GRIP OF DREAMBERRY
UPOR, UNTIL--
SPLOOSH!
WAKE UP, YOU MANGY ELF! UP WITH YOU!
YOUR MOANIN' AND GROANIN'S ENOUGH TO CURL OUR WATER-PILLARS!
RRAAAWW-GHRPH! *GURGLE*
AS BEARCLAW DRAGS HIMSELF GROGGILY TOWARD THE SURFACE, DIM FEARS NAG AT HIM.
AGH, BEAR DUNG! SUN IS LIKE DAGGERS IN MY EYES.
SHOULDN'T HAVE TAKEN THAT LAST GULP.
HOW LONG WAS I OUT THIS TIME?
HALF-REMEMBERED NIGHTMARES.
A FORMLESS SENSE OF DREAD.
SHORTLY, AS HE ARRIVES AT THE HOLT...
WELL, WHAT ARE YOU STARING AT?
THIS HEAD I'VE GOT IS LESSON ENOUGH! I--
HUH...?

WHAT IS IT, TREESTUMP? TELL ME!
RAIN'S BEEN WORKING ON 'IM DAY AND NIGHT, BUT--
WORKING... ON WHO?!
OH HIGH ONES...!
NOT MY CUB...?!
MY CUB!!
JOYLEAF! WHAT HAPP--
-- I SENT AND SENT...
YOU DIDN'T ANSWER.

CHOKE TELL ME HE WILL *LIVE*, HEALER.
CUTTER HAS HIS SIRE'S STRENGTH... AND HIS MOTHER'S HEART...
ELSE I'D HAVE FAILED.

BEARCLAW EMERGES FROM THE FATHER TREE TO FACE HIS TRIBE'S SILENT CENSURE.

STIFF-LIPPED, HE HEARS TREESTUMP'S TERSE ACCOUNT OF *BROWNBERRY* AND *FOXFUR'S* NARROW ESCAPE...

...AND OF WHAT BEFELL AFTER.

SO CUTTER TOOK INTO HIS HEAD TO GO *TALK* TO THE HUMANS... TRY TO MAKE *PEACE*.

YOU KNOW THE REST.

IN EVERY SOLEMN FACE...
...IN EACH OWL-LIKE PAIR OF UNBLINKING EYES...
...ONE UNSPOKEN ACCUSATION...
"WHERE WERE YOU, OUR CHIEF, WHEN YOUR SON..."
"WHEN WE ALL NEEDED YOU?"
THOUGH THEY CANNOT-- WOULD NOT -- SLAY HIM, TO BEARCLAW, THIS MOMENT...
...WHEN EVEN THE MOST LOYAL OF THE LOYAL WILL NOT MEET HIS EYES...
...IS MORE PAINFUL BY FAR.
RRRUMMBLE
IT WAS... THE DRINK!
BUT THE BLAME IS ALL MINE

SO BEGINS A RITUAL THAT HAS UNITED THE TRIBE THROUGH GOOD TIMES AND BAD...
ON MY SON'S BLOOD -- AND MY OWN -- I MAKE THIS VOW...
...I WILL NEVER FAIL YOU AGAIN!
...WITH ONE HEART AND ONE MIND, SINCE THE REIGN OF...
...TIMMORN YELLOW-EYES...
RAHNEE THE SHE-WOLF...
...PREY-PACER...
...TWO-SPEAR...
...HUNTRESS SKYFIRE... ...FREEFOOT...
...TANNER... ...GOODTREE...
...MANTRICKER...
BEARCLAW!
THAT'S BETTER THAN I DESERVE, WOLFRIDERS.
NOW, I ENTREAT YOU, ALLOW ME TO GO OFF ONE MORE TIME ALONE.
LET ME FULFILL WHAT MY SON BEGAN...
MY SON WHO IS SO MUCH WISER THAN I.

AND... WITH THE TRIBE'S ASSENT...
RRRRRUMMMBLE-RUMMMM
GO, BLACKFELL, GO!
A WHILE LATER, IN THE HUMANS' CAMP...
‹ YOU HEAR, TABAK? GOTARA GRUMBLES FROM THE SKY! ›
KRAK-KRUMMM!
‹ WE SHOULD NOT HAVE FAILED! IT WAS THE SWIFT DEMON-WOLVES! ›
‹ IF NOT FOR THEM, WE'D HAVE SLAIN THEIR FEMALE RIDERS! ›
YOU WANT "DEMONS," ROUND-EARS?
THEN, COME FOR ME!
GRRRRRR...
‹ HAAIIEE!! AFTER HIM! ›
‹ NO! WAIT! IT IS A TRICK! ›
THE ENRAGED, YOUTHFUL HUNTERS DO NOT HEED.
BEARCLAW LEADS THEM DEEP INTO THE FOREST.
HENH HENH. THAT'S GOT 'E CHASING THE OWN TAILS!

<TABAK! *PANT PANT* COME BACK! COME BACK!!>
"AND I TRUST BLACKFELL TO BRING MY TRUE PREY..."
"... WHERE WE MAY MEET ON ISOLATED GROUND."
< AAAGH! TH-THE BLACK WOLF! >
< SERVANT OF THE DEMON-CHIEF HIMSELF! >
GRRRR-RRRROOOWWWRRRR
KRA-BOOOOOM!
THE MASTER SPIRIT POUNDS HIS SKY-DRUM AND THROWS HIS SKY-FIRE...
< AHHH! GOTARA, SAVE ME! >
KRAK!
... YET THE SHADOW-BEAST DRIVES THE SHAMAN EVER DEEPER INTO AN UNKNOWN PART OF THE WOODS WHERE...

...BEARCLAW STANDS WAITING, OPEN-HANDED, OBLIVIOUS TO THE STORM BREAKING OVERHEAD.
KRAKKOW!
<HUMAN CHIEF! IT IS TIME WE TALK!>
<THE FOREST IS WIDE AND GAME IS PLENTIFUL. THERE IS ENOUGH FOR BOTH OUR TRIBES.>
<WE MUST FIND A WAY TO LIVE TOGETHER IN PEACE.>
<NEVER! YOU HAVE NO PLACE HERE, DEMON!>
<WE WILL CLEANSE THE LAND OF YOU!>
RATTLE RATTLE!
UNNOTICED, BLACKFELL DETECTS AN ANCIENT RESIDUE...
<THIS IS OUR FOREST, BY THE BLESSING OF GOTARA WHO SENT US THE SACRED BEAR!>
SNIFF SNIFF *WHINE*

< WHY DO YOU BELIEVE SUCH THINGS? >
< A BEAR IS A BEAR! AND I KILLED THAT ONE! >
< YOU SHOULD THANK ME FOR LETTING YOU KEEP IT! >
RRRRUMMMMMBLLE-KRAKKK!
< LIES! DEMON LIES! YOU ARE AN EVIL MONSTER! >
< YOU KILLED MY ELDER, MY SHAMAN-TEACHER WHO WAS A FATHER TO ME! >
< YOU AND YOUR KIND ARE THE MONSTERS! >
< YOU'VE KILLED MY FRIENDS... MY TRIBE'S CHILDREN! >
< AND YOU ALMOST KILLED MY SON! >
< I SHOULD'VE KNOWN THIS WAS HOPELESS! YOU'RE MEAT TO BE WASTED! >
MMF *MMF* *MMF*
< YOU DIE NOW, DEMON!! >
BLINDED AND DEAFENED AGAIN BY HATE, MAN AND ELF DO NOT HEAR THE WOLF'S AGITATED WHINES.
THEY CANNOT SEE, AS THE WOLF CAN, WHAT THEIR VIOLENT EMOTIONS HAVE AWAKENED...

...A POOL OF ***ELFIN MAGIC*** THAT HAS LAIN ***STAGNANT*** FOR EONS -- MAGIC GONE ***BAD!***

GRAAAAARRRRRRR!!

THEY DO NOT FEEL THE INVISIBLE TENDRILS REACHING OUT FOR THEM IN NEWFOUND ***HUNGER...***

...LUSTING AFTER THE ***RAGE*** AND ***HATRED*** THEY HAVE FULLY UNLEASHED!

SUDDENLY, BEFORE THE FATAL BLOWS CAN BE STRUCK...

〈 DIIIIEEEEEE!!! 〉
OOOWWWW...

UUUHHHH...
< OOHHHH... >
TSSSSSSSSS
FRANTICALLY, BLACKFELL DRAGS HIS ELF-FRIEND AWAY FROM THE QUESTING TENDRILS...
SO, TOO, THE HUMAN SOURCE OF SUSTENANCE ESCAPES THE SINISTER MAGIC'S LIMITED GRASP.
THE LIGHTNING HAS FUELED IT, BUT NOT ENOUGH.
IT REACHES OUT, SEEKING WHAT HAS ELUDED IT, SEEKING WHAT IT NEEDS TO LIVE...
...MORE RAGE AND HATRED!
AND SO THEY COME - ANCIENT ENEMIES - CAT AND SNAKE, THEIR NATURAL ANIMOSITY HEIGHTENED BY THE MAGIC'S PULL.

HHHHISSSSSSST!
RRRROOOOAARRRR!
THE MAGIC ENTWINES THEM IN THEIR DEATH STRUGGLE...
...FEEDING ON THEIR RAW PAIN AND RAGE...
...MERGING... CHANGING UNTIL...

KRAKATHOOOM!
KTOOM!
...MADCOIL IS BORN!

AT FIRST IT HUNTS SMALL GAME...
chirp chirp chirp
chitter chitter
GRRRRRR-RRRRUUURRRRR...
SHRIEEEKK!!
...NEVER STRAYING FROM ITS CURSED CORNER OF THE FOREST...
...UNTIL THERE IS NONE LEFT.
THEN THE QUARRY GROWS LARGER...
RRRREEEEEEE! RRREEEEEEEE!
...AND LARGER STILL AS THE MONSTER GROWS...

...ALONG WITH ITS MONSTROUS APPETITE!
< WE HAVE COME TOO FAR. I DO NOT LIKE IT. >
< IT IS SO ... SO STILL! >
< NO BIRDS... NO CHATTER OF SQUIRRELS. >
< AN EVIL DEMON PLACE! LET US GO BACK... >
< ...NOW! >
BUT CAUTION COMES TOO LATE!
ROOOOWWWWWLLLLLL!
SHRAAAKK!!
GYAAAAAAH!!
AAAAAAAHHHH!
AAAAIIEEEE!!

AT THE EDGE OF HIS TRIBE'S CAMP, INSIDE A SMALL MUD AND SKIN LODGE BUILT FOUR TURNS OF THE SEASONS AGO...
...THE SHAMAN *SWEATS.*
AFTER THE LIGHTNING BOLT STRUCK, HE USED THE HOVEL FOR *HEALING.*
SINCE THEN, HIS SOUL HAS BEEN TROUBLED.
MANY LONG DAYS HAS HE SPENT IN FUTILE MEDITATION.
‹ OH MIGHTY GOTARA, THE DEMONS HIDE WELL FROM US. ›
‹ THERE HAS BEEN PEACE. AND I... ›
‹ ...I HAVE DONE *NOTHING!* ›
SSSHHHSSSSSHHHH
‹ WHEN YOU HURLED YOUR BURNING SKY-SPEAR DOWN UPON THE TWO OF US... ›
THUMP!
‹ ...WHY DID YOU *SPARE* THE DEMON-CHIEF? *WHY? WHY??* ›
‹ ARE THEY *NOT* YOUR *ENEMIES,* HE AND HIS TRIBE...? ›
‹ TELL ME, MASTER OF ALL SPIRITS, I *BEG* YOU! ›
‹ SEND A *SIGN* TO YOUR MOST FAITHFUL SERVANT! ›
COUNTLESS TIMES HAS HIS CRY GONE UP.

TODAY HE IS ANSWERED!
SHAMAN! MY SHAMAN, COME SEE!
< TABAK...WAS IT A LONGTOOTH? >
< IT WAS... IT WAS DEMON MAGIC! >
< "YOKUT TOLD US OF A MONSTER BEFORE HE DIED." >
< ...TAIL OF SNAKE... LONGTOOTH'S HEAD... BIGGER THAN TALL ROCK..>
< *GUHHHH...* >
< "THERE WAS DEMON STENCH ALL AROUND. WE FOUND BITS OF THE OTHER MEN'S BLOOD AND SKIN." >
< "AND TRACKS OF SNAKE AND LONGTOOTH TOGETHER -- BIG! -- JUST AS YOKUT SAID!" >

< PRAISE YOU, GOTARA! >
< HERE, AT LAST, IS PROOF THE DEMON-CHIEF WHO OFFERED US PEACE LIED! >
< HE AND HIS EVIL TRIBE HIDE, USING FOUL MAGIC TO GROW A MONSTROUS BEAST TO PREY ON US! >
< YES, YES! ONLY DEMONS CAN TWIST AND SHAPE CREATURES TO DO THEIR WILL. >
< TONIGHT WE DANCE TO THE DRUMS OF DEATH! >
< FROM NOW ON, WE EXIST WITH BUT ONE PURPOSE... >
< ...SEARCH THE FOREST 'TIL WE FIND THE DEMONS' LAIR... >
< ...AND WIPE THEM FROM THE FACE OF THE WORLD! >
RUM TA-TA-TUM'TUM TA-TA-RUM TUM TUM

FOR FOUR TURNS OF THE SEASONS, THE HUMANS HAVE LEFT THE ELVES ALONE. THE FARAWAY RUMBLE OF THEIR DRUMS, NOW, CAUSES NO STIR IN THE TRANQUIL HOLT...
EVER SINCE BEARCLAW RETURNED TO HIS DEN WITH SKYFIRE-CRISPED FLESH ABOUT WHICH HE WOULD NOT SPEAK, THE WOLFRIDER CHIEF HAS KEPT HIS VOW.
HE IS MORE THOUGHTFUL, LESS QUICK TO ANGER.
HIS DEVOTION TO HIS TRIBE IS GREATER THAN IT HAS EVER BEEN.
NO MORE LONE EXCURSIONS ON ERRANDS OF MISCHIEF..AND NOT SO MUCH AS A DROP OF THE TROLLS' DREAMBERRY WINE.
AT LONG LAST, THE OLD BADGER HAS FOUND HAPPINESS IN THE HEART OF HIS FAMILY --
-- LEAVING ROOM FOR A MATURING SON TO EXPLORE THE MYSTERIES OF LIFE...AND LOVE.

TROLL GAMES AND SOUL NAMES
DEEP NIGHT...SULTRY NIGHT...THE ANCIENT FOREST MURMURS, MOIST AND ASTIR WITH LIFE SEEKING, IN MYRIAD WAYS, TO RENEW ITSELF.
IN THE DANCE OF SEDUCTION, SOME WIN, SOME LOSE. FEELING MOCKED BY THE FEVERISH HUM AND THRUM ALL AROUND HIM...
...A YOUTH OF FOURTEEN TURNS OF THE SEASONS TRUDGES FROM HIS PLAY-MATE'S DEN, DISSATISFIED AND BROODING.
STORY: SONNY STRAIT, WENDY & RICHARD PINI
PENCILS AND INKS: SONNY STRAIT
ART DIRECTION, SCRIPT & LETTERS: WENDY PINI

HEY, CUTTER!
WHAT'S DOING, CUB?
....
WON'T TALK...?
YOU AND NIGHTFALL HAVING TOO MUCH FUN FOR WORDS, EH?
DON'T START, SKYWISE!
SHRUMPF!
OOF! WHAT'S THIS? A SOUR NOTE IN THE SONG OF BUDDING PLAY?
DON'T WORRY! IT TAKES TIME TO BECOME EXPERT AT ANY GAME!
IT'S NOT THAT! I JUST...I DON'T LIKE LIMITS!
THE ANSWERS...THE TRUTH ...RIGHT TO THE CORE! I WANNA CUT TO 'EM - NOW!
I WANNA BE THE SEED, THE ROOTS, THE TREE, THE BRANCHES, THE LEAVES, THE FRUIT... AND THE SEED AGAIN.
SIGH
PUCKERNUTS! IT'S GREAT TO BE CURIOUS --
-- BUT ONLY IF THERE'S FUN TO BE HAD!
WHY SO GLUM THESE DAYS?
BECAUSE SOMEDAY...I'LL BE CHIEF.
AND I HAVE TO BE A GOOD AND WISE ONE.

OF COURSE! HOLD CUTTER, LOOD OF TEN CHIEFS!
HUNTER, LEADER --
-- AND TIRELESS PLEASER OF EVERY MAIDEN IN WOLFRIDER TERRITORY!
GRRRR!
HEY! WHA --?!
EEYOWW!
WHISSSHHH!
HUUNH!!
RRRGH!
KRUMPF!
HEH HEH...
YOU'VE CUT YOUR MILK TEETH, THAT'S SURE!

BUT I'VE GOT A GOOD BITE, MYSELF!
AAACK!!
GNRRGH!
QUIT IT QUIT IT QUIT IT!!
YOU...YOU TROLL-FACED FISH POKER!
COUNTLESS BEAKED, BUGGY AND BEASTLY LOVE MATCHES ARE RUDELY INTERRUPTED...
CAW
CAW
CRACKLE
SHRIEEK!
...AS THE STARGAZER ZIGZAGS THROUGH THE UNDERGROWTH, UNABLE TO SHAKE HIS ENRAGED PURSUER.
CHITTER
CHITTER
SUDDENLY...
WOOPS!
PANT PANT GOOD MOVES, CUB!
CORNERED! NOW WHO'S GOT WHO?!
QUIT CALLING ME THAT!

LOOK... COOL OFF! I DIDN'T MEAN --
-- I KNOW. SORRY.
JUST LEAVE ME ALONE!
IN THIS MOOD? RIGHT!
PANT PANT
MMM MMMF?
STARJUMPER...! NIGHTRUNNER! SNIFFED US OUT, EH?
C'MON. LET'S SEE WHAT THAT BURR UNDER HIS TAIL'S REALLY ABOUT.
OLDER THAN CUTTER, THOUGH NOT BY FAR, SKYWISE KNOWS WELL TO LET THE SILENCE LINGER...
THROUGH STARLIGHT AND CLOUD, THUNDER AND SNOW, THIS IS THE HILLTOP WHERE COMMUNION BEGINS WITH WORDS, BUT OFTEN GOES DEEPER...
IT'S NIGHTFALL...
SHE-SHE SAID I WAS GETTING TOO NEAR ...HER SOUL NAME!
SHE PUSHED ME AWAY --

-- JUST WHEN I FELT THIS CLOSE TO FINDING --
-- TO KNOWING ALL ABOUT --
-- RECOGNITION!
OH... THAT!
"LOVEMATES JOIN FOR PLEASURE, LIFEMATES JOIN FOR LOVE. BUT RECOGNITION ...AH!"
DON'T JOKE!
PLAYING IS FUN, BUT...
...THERE'S SO MUCH MORE! I FEEL IT INSIDE!
AWW, RECOGNITION JUST MAKES NUTMASH OF A SIMPLE DELIGHT, CUB!
WE'D ALL BE BETTER OFF WITHOUT IT!
HUH?! IS YOUR SHELL CRACKED? WE'D DIE OUT!
TRUE. GUESS THAT'S WHAT RECOGNITION'S FOR...MAKIN' MORE PESKY, LITTLE ANKLE-BITERS.
BUT...ISN'T IT ALSO BEING SO CLOSE TO ANOTHER --
-- THAT YOU SHARE EVERYTHING... EVEN YOUR --
-- SOUL NAME?
SO I HEAR. HASN'T HAPPENED TO ME, YET. AND IF I'M LUCKY...
YOU DON'T WANT IT?!
NOPE. DON'T WANT ANYONE'S SOUL TIED TO MINE.
WANNA BE JUST WHAT I AM...FREE AND HAP --

SNIFF
-- BEARCLAW!
YOU DO ANYTHING TO SET HIS EARS BACK?
NO...WHY?
'CUZ HE'S ON THE PROWL! C'MON!
FATHER... IN THIS PART OF THE WOODS... ALONE...?
KEEP DOWN! THE OLD BADGER'S GOT THREE NOSES AND SIX EARS!
I'M WORRIED. HE PROMISED US ALL HE'D NEVER --
-- GET MIXED UP WITH THE TROLLS AGAIN.
THEN, WHAT...?
LET'S KEEP AN EYE ON 'IM!
BET HE'S CAUGHT OUR SCENT ALREADY! HE'S GONNA KILL US!
IF HE CATCHES US! BESIDES...WHO WAS IT, A WHILE AGO, WANTED TO KNOW EVERYTHING?

SOON...
KLANNG! KLANNG! KTANG!
OPEN UP, TROLLS!
I-I CAN'T BELIEVE IT! HE PROMISED --
-- HE'D NEVER GO DRINKING AND PLAYING TOSS-STONE AGAIN!
WAIT! GIVE HIM A CHANCE!
CR-R-R-EEEAK!
WELL, WELL! THE WOLFRIDER CHIEF! IT'S BEEN QUITE A STRETCH!
WIPE YOUR FEET - AND DON'T BRING ANY TICKS IN WITH YOU, THIS TIME!
NO, SCURFF. THIS IS UNFINISHED BUSINESS. GIVE ME WHAT'S RIGHTFULLY MINE --
-- THAT RING! IT'S TO BE A BRACELET FOR MY LIFEMATE. I WON IT FAIR! YOU AND YOUR KING KNOW IT!
HAND IT OVER, AND WE'RE QUITS!
HUNH! I REMEMBER THAT GAME...AND THAT BAUBLE.
YOURS, YOU SAY? GREYMUNG GAVE IT TO HIS FAVORITE.
TAKE IT UP WITH HIM!

NO! I PROMISED MY TRIBE I'D NEVER SET FOOT INSIDE YOUR FOUL ANTHILL AGAIN.
THEN, THAT'S TOO BAD FOR YOU, ISN'T IT?
GRRRR-RRR!
TSK TSK POOR LITTLE ELF CHIEF.
THE SLEEP FURS'LL BE COLD FOR YOU, TONIGHT, WON'T THEY? *SNICKER*
CR-R-R-EEEAK!
SLAM!
COME, BLACKFELL... BACK TO THE HOLT.
SNIFF SNIFF
I KNOW YOU'RE THERE, MY EXPERT THIEF OF BIRD EGGS AND FORBIDDEN BERRIES.
ARE YOU, ON YOUR OWN, UP TO SNATCHING --
-- THIS?
BY ALL THE STARS!
???

HEE HEE HEE!
GO ON HOME, CUB. I HAVE WORK TO DO --
-- FOR YOUR SIRE!
SURE. WHY SHOULDN'T YOU PUSH ME AWAY --

-- LIKE EVERYONE ELSE?

AW, WAIT! YOU'RE SICK OF BEING TREATED LIKE A PUP, AREN'T YOU?
YOU MIGHT JUST BE USEFUL AT THAT.

BESIDES, THERE'S NO REAL DANGER.
GETTING PAST THE TROLLS'LL BE EASIER THAN WALKING A TREE BRANCH!

WHAT'RE WE AFTER?
JUST FOLLOW MY LEAD!
KRING
KLINNG
KLING

CREEE-EEEE-EEEK
...WORMWATER AND NOSE-HAIR KNOTS...! MISERABLE ELVES GOT NO MANNERS AT ALL!
AWAY, OR I'LL SIC THE GUARDS ON YOU!
OWL PELLETS! NO TROLL BORN EVER SETS FOOT OUTSIDE!
BEARCLAW'S TOO DIGNIFIED TO HAGGLE WITH THE LIKES OF YOU!
HE SENT US IN HIS PLACE.
I'M BEARCLAW'S SON, CUTTER. I DEMAND TO SEE KING GREYMUNG.
WELL PLAYED!
THIS IS AN UNPLEASANT TWIST!
IF WE REFUSE, IT COULD AFFECT TRADE WITH THE ELVES HEREAFTER.
HMPH! GUESS I BETTER REPORT TO GREYMUNG.
AS LONG MOMENTS DRAG BY...
WE'LL GET IN. REMEMBER, DON'T LET 'EM SEE YOU ANXIOUS.
BE CALM... IN CHARGE.
YOU'RE BEARCLAW'S CUB, AREN'T YOU?
RIGHT... CALM...IN CHARGE...!

MEANWHILE, IN SUBTERRANEAN DEPTHS BEYOND EVEN THE ELVES' SUPERB HEARING...
HEH HEH... YESSS...
ODDBIT, MY BOUNTIFUL TREASURE! SPARKLE AND SHINE!
JING-TINGA TING
JINGA JING
BOOM BADA BOOM BOOM
BOOM BADA BOOM
JINGA JING JING
AMAZINGLY LIGHT FOOTED, THE DANCER TWIRLS, DISPLAYING ALL HER ASSETS --
-- TO BEST ADVANTAGE.
WELL...? WHAT'RE YOU GAWPING AT?
UH...

ER...EH, AHEM!
TWO ELVES ABOVE, MY KING. ONE CLAIMS TO BE BEARCLAW'S SON.
THEY-THEY HAVE SOME DISPUTE OVER - YOUR PARDON - LOVELY ODDBIT'S RING.
WHAT OF IT?
THEY DEMAND AN AUDIENCE.
RING...? RING...?!
OOOH, NO! IT'S MINE FOR KEEPS!
YOU SAID SO, MUNGY! SEND THE NASTY ELVES AWAY!
AH, "NECTAR NUBS," YOUR MASTER HAS A MUCH BETTER IDEA. THOSE LITTLE, PINK SLUGS DARE QUESTION MY GAMING HONOR, EH?
THAT MEANS I HAVE EVERY RIGHT TO HOLD 'EM AND DEMAND REDRESS FOR THE INSULT!
FETCH 'EM DOWN, PICKNOSE.
OVERSTUFFED, OVERINDULGED, EARRING-RIDDLED OLD RUSTBALL...!
SOMETHIN' STINKS...AND I BET THE ONE WHO ENDS UP STEPPIN' IN IT'LL BE -- ME!
EQUALLY DOUBTFUL OF GREYMUNG'S PLAN, SCURFF TURNS THE DEVICE, SWINGING THE GREAT, STONE DOOR WIDE.
GASP!
WHAT IS THAT?!
NEVER MIND! KING GREYMUNG'S GRACIOUSLY AGREED TO SEE YOU. GET YER SCRAWNY TAILS IN HERE!

BLINDFOLDS?! PRETTY INSULTING, PICKNOSE!
DON'T YOU TRUST US?
VERY FUNNY. QUIT WRIGGLIN'!
YOU CAN TRUST US, Y'KNOW.
WE'RE NOT HERE TO BREAK ANY RULES.
YOU ALREADY HAVE! ONLY BEARCLAW WAS EVER WELCOME BELOW!
THOUGH LED SIGHTLESS, THE ELVES' KEENLY CURIOUS NOSES AND EARS TELL THEM MUCH OF THEIR SURROUNDINGS...
...REMEMBER, TOO, WE'VE BEEN LIVING UNDER THE FOREST AGES LONGER THAN YOU WOLFRIDERS HAVE LIVED IN IT!
BY RIGHTS, IT'S OUR TERRITORY!
UH HUH...FULL OF FEROCIOUS BEASTS AND HUMANS! YOU'RE WELCOME TO VISIT ...ANYTIME!
SMARTY-BREECHES
FORTUNATELY, CUTTER CANNOT SEE THE SHEER PLUNGE FROM THE PRECIPITOUS STAIR...
BUT, BY A RISING CURRENT OF SULPHUROUS AIR --
-- SKYWISE GAUGES THE DISTANCE AND...
CUTTER! BLINDFOLD OFF! JUMP!
NOW!!
JUMP -- ?!? AAAUGH!
HEY! YOU SNEAKY -- !!

IS ISN'T
RIGHT!
SCURFF! SOUND THE ALARM!
NO --
KLANNG!
KLANNG!
KLANNG!
-- BUT IT'S NECESSARY -- OOF!!
WE PROMISED!!
KLANNG!
KLANNG!
SOMETIMES YOU GOTTA BEND THE TRUTH, CUB --
-- TO GET WHAT YOU WANT!
HURRY! STAY WITH ME!
KLANNG!
PANT PANT BUT WE'RE SUPPOSED --
EEEEK!!
-- TO DO THIS HONORABLY!
BEARCLAW CHARGED ME TO GET THE RING - BY ANY MEANS!
BUT WHAT IF THE TROLL KING REALLY DID WIN IT FAIR?

NOT LIKELY! BEARCLAW'S A BETTER PLAYER! GREYMUNG MUST'VE PULLED A REAL --
-- HELLO?!
KLANNG!
THE RING! JUST AS BEARCLAW SHOWED ME!
TOLD YOU THIS'D BE EASY!
KLANNG!
YAWN
I'M WORN TO A SHADOW, GRANDMAMA!
WE'LL BE BACK IN THE HOLT IN TWO TWITCHES OF A WOLF'S TAIL!
KLANNG!
KLANNG!
...MUNGY MADE ME DANCE MY POOR TOESIES RAW!
HAMMERS AND TONGS! WHAT DO YOU SUPPOSE IS GOING ON OUT THERE?
KLANNG!
NOTHING SERIOUS, CHILD. *CACKLE*
KLANNG!
KLANNG!
THE MENFOLK BANG THE BARS WHEN A MOUSE SQUIRTS IN THE PANTRY!
WELL, *SIGH* NOT EVEN THE ALARM WILL KEEP ME AWAKE --
-- ONCE I HIT THE CUSHIONS!
WIGGLE WIGGLE
KLANNG!
PUCKERNUTS! I'VE SEEN "BARE..."
...BUT NOT THAT BARE!

FINALLY, THE ALARM DIES DOWN AND...
I THINK SHE'S ASLEEP!
ZZZNNOOORRRR
ZZZZRRRRRRZZZZZ
ZZZNAAAAAZZZZ
GO! WE'LL SNATCH THE RING AND FOLLOW OUR OWN SCENT OUT OF HERE!
I STILL DON'T LIKE THIS!
THEN STAND BACK AND WATCH AN EXPERT HUNTER CLOSE IN ON HIS PREY!
ZZZZZZ...
SKILLFULLY... DELICATELY...
MMMRRM *GRRMPH...*
FLOOP!
ZZZNOORRR...
CAREFUL! DO IT SLOWLY... GENTLY...!
OH, DUNG!
IT'S STUCK!!
THUD!

EEEEEEK!!
YAAAAAH!!
ODDBIT...?
WHADDAYA MEAN, "THEY GOT AWAY?!" LOOKA THIS MESS!
KONK!
ODDBIT!!
I'M COMING!
I'M HERE, MY L -- *GLORP!*
OOO! EEEEE! OO GET AWAY GET AWA
BLUMP!
GOTTA GET THAT RING!

MY RING!! PICKY! DO SOMETHING!!
DUUUHH...
POP!
SHWIPP!
AYOOOAH!

HAH!
OOUGH!! S-SKYWISE!! HELLLLPH!
BLUMPF!
C'MERE, WORM!
YEEOOF!
!!! TROLLS GOT REAL ROCKS DOWN THERE?

KONK!
UNGH!!

TOOK YOU LONG ENOUGH! LET GREYMUNG HAVE 'EM NOW!
YEAH! AND WHEN HE'S DONE --
I'M STUFFIN' A BELLOWS UP THIS ONE'S NETHER PIPE!
HEH HEH...

SOON...
SO...THOUGHT YOU'D TRICK ME, EH?! ROB ME, EH? SLIP IN AND OUT EASY AS HOT OIL, EH?
HOW DARE YOU FLOUT MY AUTHORITY, YOU SQUEEDLY LITTLE THIEVES!?
YOU'LL PAY DEARLY FOR THIS AFFRONT! THE RING! WHERE IS IT?
TALK!

YOU HEARD! OBEY THE KING!
MMM? UM MUN'T MUH.
SLAM!
BWUH-HUH!
WHAT PUNISHMENT, GREAT ONE?
WAIT! JUST SWEAR YOU WON THE RING FAIRLY!
NO, ROCK SKULL!!
HMMMM...
THIS ONE'S HONEST, GULLIBLE... NOTHING LIKE HIS FATHER.
OF COURSE I SWEAR...ON MY HONOR AS A TROLL!
THEN, AS BEARCLAW'S SON, I TAKE FULL RESPONSIBILITY --
-- FOR BREAKING TROLL LAW!
PUNISH ME!
DISGUSTINGLY NOBLE, BUT USELESS, ELF. YOU'RE BOTH MY SLAVES!
YOU FLUFF-HEADED DUPE! LOOK WHAT YOU'VE GOTTEN US INTO!
ONLY A FOOL PLAYS BY THEIR RULES! TROLLS HAVEN'T A DROP OF TRUTH OR HONOR IN 'EM!
WHO SAYS, YOU MISERABLE WISP?!
WE TROLLS HAVE GREAT HONOR ...ESPECIALLY WHEN IT COMES TO A GAME WE INVENTED!

WELL, IF THAT'S SO --

-- THEN *WE* WERE WRONG AND WE NEED TO MAKE *AMENDS.*

YOU'RE OUT OF YOUR *DREAMBERRY-PICKIN'* *MIND,* YOU KNOW THAT?!

!!!

SO GO TO *BEARCLAW* AND GROWL WITH *HIM* ABOUT MY ROCK-SKULLNESS 'TIL THE *MOONS MELT!*

YOU SEE, *GREYMUNG...* I COULD'VE ESCAPED *ANYTIME.*

BUT I *PROMIS* I WON'T GIVE YO ANY TROUBLE -

-- IF YOU L *SKYWISE* G

WHY FEED *TWO* MOUTHS WHEN *ONE'S* ENOUGH? ESPECIALLY *THIS* ONE - *BEARCLAW'S* *WHELP!*

THOSE *WOLFRIDERS'LL* DO *ANYTHING* TO KEEP HIM SAFE! NO MORE TRADES... JUST *TRIBUTE!* I CAN *MILK 'EM DRY!*

ALL RIGHT! THE *RING-SWALLOWER* GOES FREE!

AN ALL-WISE CHIEF, SOMEDAY, HUH?! WELL, YOU'RE *TOO TRUSTING FOR YOUR OWN GOOD!*

THAT'S WHY *BEARCLAW* GAVE *ME* THE RING TASK --

-- HE KNEW YOU'D MUCK IT HOPELESS!

UNCEREMONIOUSLY SHOVED OUT INTO THE PRE-DAWN WOODS, SKYWISE FINDS THE WOLVES ANXIOUSLY WAITING...
SIGH
C'MON... NOTHING MORE WE CAN DO, HERE.

SKRITCH
SNIFF *SNIFF* *SNIFF*
SKRITCH
MMMMH MMMMH MMMMMmm!

NO NIGHTRUNNER, HE --
-- HE'S NOT COMING HOME WITH US.

LESS THAN EAGER, THE YOUTHFUL STARGAZER TAKES HIS TIME WENDING HOLTWARD...
SO QUIET...!
EVERYONE'S TURNED IN FOR THE DAY.
GUESS I BETTER WAKE BEARCLAW AND JOYLEAF...
...AND GET IT OVER WITH.

SHORTLY...
...THEY WON'T HURT HIM. BUT THEY WON'T RELEASE HIM EITHER.
HE'S THEIR SLAVE.
YOUNG FOOL! HOW COULD YOU LET IT HAPPEN?!
EXPLORING THE TROLL CAVES WITHOUT LEAVE...INEXCUSABLE!
LIFEMATE YOUR TON BETRAYS YOU...!
YOU BOTH KNOW MORE OF THIS THAN YOU'RE TELLING.
HIS DAY SPENT IN SLEEPLESS DREAD, SKYWISE MEEKLY FACES THE TRIBE...
OF ALL THE WITLESS, POINTLESS STUNTS TO PULL -- !
CUTTER LOOKS UP TO YOU! YOU KNEW HE'D FOLLOW YOU!!
YOU KNEW, TOO, MY CHIEF.
THIS ISN'T FAIR! I ONLY DID WHAT YOU ASKED!
TIME ENOUGH TO LAY BLAME LATER! I SAY MOUNT UP AND RESCUE THE LAD -- NOW
AYE!
....
TREESTUMP'S RIGHT! THE TROLLS HAVE GONE TOO FAR! LET'S TEACH THEM A LESSON!

NO ONE WANTS THAT
E THAN *I!* BUT THE TROLLS
HAVE THE *NUMBERS* --

"SO LONG AS THEY HAVE HIM, THE TROLLS HAVE US *HOBBLED!* MUCH AS WE HATE IT, WE MUST DEAL FOR MY SON ON *THEIR TERMS!*"

-- *AND* THE HIGH-WROUGHT DEFENSES! WE'RE *TOO FEW* AND TOO *LIGHTLY-ARMED* TO FREE *CUTTER* BY FORCE.

GRUMBLE

DON'T GLARE AT *ME,* TRIBEMATES. I'M NOT THE *ONLY* ONE TO BLAME!

THE FOLLOWING NIGHT...
ER...THAT'S ALL RIGHT, CUB, WE HAVE PLENTY ENOUGH HUNTERS, TONIGHT.
RIGHT.

AND THE NIGHT AFTER...
FOXFUR...? WANNA GO VISIT THE DREAMBERRY PATCH?
SOME OTHER TIME. I'VE GOT ARROWHEADS TO SHARPEN.

UH...
CUB...?
THANKS FOR KEEPING... THE TRUTH... JUST BETWEEN US.

OF COURSE I KNEW CUTTER WOULD GO WITH YOU. SAW IT AS AN INITIATION, OF SORTS.

JUST DIDN'T THINK HE'D BE SO HIGH HEADED - OR STUBBORN - AS TO SACRIFICE HIMSELF!

IT'S BEEN HARD, HASN'T IT?

NOT TO TELL OF YOUR PART IN IT...? YES. BUT YOU'VE DONE SO MUCH TO EARN BACK THE TRIBE'S TRUST.

I UNDERSTAND WHY THE SECRET MUST BE KEPT.

THE RING...HE DIDN'T WANT TO GET IT MY - OUR - WAY, THE TRICKY WAY. BUT I DIDN'T CARE...

...I JUST WENT ON AND TOLD HIM TO BE WHAT HE CAN NEVER BE --

BEARCLAW, THE MEAT OF IT IS --

-- I LET YOU AND CUTTER, BOTH, DOWN.

" -- A MERE FOLLOWER."
CRACK!
HEAR THE LASH, ELF?
MOVE FASTER OR I'LL REALLY USE IT ON YOU.
UUUH-HNGH!
YEAH! GET THE BRICKS OUTTA YOUR BREECHES, PINK-SKIN!
WHY'D THEY STICK US WITH THAT WEAK-LING, ANYWAY?!
SECRETED BEYOND SENDING RANGE, THE ELF YOUTH PERFORMS HIS LOWLY TASKS IN SILENCE...ALWAYS LISTENING...LEARNING...
...SO WHATTA YA THINK HE DOES WHEN HE SPOTS THAT FIRE-EYE STONE MISSIN' FROM HIS POUCH? HE...
...FORMING IMPRESSIONS OF A SOCIETY OBSESSED WITH COMFORT AND GAIN...A SOCIETY VASTLY DIFFERENT FROM HIS OWN --
SCRAPE SCRAPE
-- BUT NOT ALTOGETHER.
FOR WOLFRIDERS, TOO, KNOW LIVING IS MORE THAN BARE SURVIVAL. THEY, TOO, PRIZE CERTAIN POSSESSIONS... ONLY NEVER, EVER AT ANOTHER TRIBEMATE'S EXPENSE.
...AND MORE OF THAT WHITETREE BARK, ROLLED, AND --
HOLD, OLD MAGGOTY! THE MOONS HAVE CHANGED MANY TIMES.
WE'VE MORE THAN MET YOUR KING'S GREEDY DEMANDS!
HOW ABOUT LETTING THE LAD GO, NOW?
AS USUAL, THE HAG SMIRKS AND PURSUES HER SYMBOL-DRAWN LIST.

AND, BECAUSE THE WOLFRIDERS VALUE A CAPTIVE TRIBESMAN'S LIFE ABOVE ALL, THE ENDLESS RANSOM CONTINUES TO BE PAID.
IT'S YOUR OWN FAULT!
I CAN'T KEEP UP WITH THE TROLLS' DEMANDS FOR MORE HIDES BY MYSELF.
IT'S THAT FOOL CUTTER'S FAULT, MOONSHADE!
HE WALKED WILLINGLY INTO THEIR SNARE.
WHOSE LEG AM I PULLING WITH HIM GON I FEEL LIKE PIECE OF ME MISSING!
"FRIEND, I REMEMBER OUR LAST TALK SO WELL."
-- ISN'T RECOGNITION ABOUT SHARING EVERYTHING?
"MAD AT ME AS YOU WERE, YOU MADE GREYMUNG LET ME GO. I COULDN'T SEE, AS THEY DRAGGED ME AWAY -- "
" -- BUT I BET YOU STOOD STRAIGHT AND TALL BEFORE HIM, LIKE THE CHIEF'S SON YOU ARE."
"YOU'VE GOT GUTS, CUB. YOU ALWAYS HAVE."
"WISH I COULD SEND HOW SORRY I AM FOR THINKING YOU NOTHING MORE -- "
" -- THAN AN ADMIRING PEST."
OH, BUT HIGH ONES! IF ONLY YOU WEREN'T SUCH AN OPEN, GUILELESS, TRUE-DEALING LITTLE DOLT!

ONE YEAR LATER...
...GOTTEN' A WHOLE LOT STRONGER... HAVETA WATCH 'IM CLOSE!
BET YOUR BIG, WARTY BUTTS YOU DO!
ZNOORRR
UNAWARE OF THE SEASONS' TURNS, CUTTER IS FAR FROM "IN THE DARK" ABOUT HIS CAPTORS' NATURES.
BAH! GREYMUNG DOESN'T REWARD US NEAR ENOUGH FOR THIS SLOP WORK.
I'D LIKE TA FLOAT THE BIG, FAT FOOL DOWN THE MUCKWAY, 'CEPT HE'D PROB'LY STICK AN' STINK UP THE TUNNELS!
HEH HEH HEH HEH
DIDJA SEE ODDBIT'S LATEST JEWEL FROM THE KING? NOW THERE'S A WENCH WHO KNOWS HOW TO GET THE BEST!
SIGH...LOOKS, WITS, AND BOOTY. WHAT MORE IN THE WORLD MATTERS?
WHAT MORE...?
HOW ABOUT LOVE, RESPECT, LOYALTY...?
LATER, IN A DARKENED CORNER OF THE PANTRY - THE ONLY PLACE CUTTER IS ALLOWED TO REMOVE HIS BLINDFOLD...
WHEN I'M CHIEF, I'LL KEEP TO "THE WAY," NO MATTER WHAT.
NO ONE WILL EVER TALK ABOUT ME BEHIND MY BACK THE WAY THEY TALK ABOUT GREYMUNG!
EXCEPT... IT LOOKS LIKE SKYWISE VALUES THINGS OVER FRIENDS.
IF MY SIRE AND MY CLOSEST FRIEND CAN THINK LIKE TROLLS...WHO CAN I EVER REALLY TRUST?

CLANG-TA-TINK
CLANG-TA-TINK
WHAT'S HE MAKING *TODAY*, *PICKY?*
A *CLEAVER* TO CUT UP ALL THE NICE *MEAT* YOUR FOLK SEND DOWN.
BET YOU'D *LOVE* TO SEE HOW WE DO IT.

I *PROMISED*...
SHSSSSSSSS

THAT'S *ONE* THING WE AGREE ON, ELF.

TO HAVE HER HEART, I'D PROMISE *ODDBIT ANYTHING* SHE WANTED - AND I'D *DELIVER!*

YOU TROLLS THINK LOVE'S A...A *THING* YOU CAN *TRADE FOR?*

*'COURSE *MUNCH*! IT'S A SIMPLE MATTER OF FAIR EXCHANGE.*

WRONG! THERE'S MORE... *MUCH* MORE!

CLANG CLANG

WHADDA YOU KNOW ABOUT IT, *SLUG?* WHO DO *YOU* LOVE?

MY PARENTS ...MY TRIBE...

I'D DO *ANYTHING* FOR THEM - FOR *NOTHING!* WE ELVES ARE *LOYAL* --

-- DO TELL! WHAT ABOUT THAT *CHUM* OF YOURS... WHATZIZNAME? THE ONE WHO GOT YOU INTO THIS?

SHSSSSS

THEN, ONE RAINY AFTERNOON...
OLD MAGGOTY! THE DREAMBERRIES WILL BE HERE ANY MOMENT!
GRUMBLE DON'T RUSH ME, YOU YOUNG MUMP! THE WEATHER'S IN MY BONES!
HEH HEH YOUR HOT DREAMBERRY WINE'LL EASE THAT! FACT IS, WE'VE ALL HAD IT POKING EASY SINCE YOU SLIPPED BEARCLAW THE "FORGETTER JUICE."
I WAS THERE! IT WAS BEAUTIFUL! ONE DROP, MID-GAME, AND THE ELF'S "LAMP" WENT OUT JUST LONG ENOUGH --
-- FOR GREYMUNG TO STEAL THAT EXTRA TOSS! *HEE HEE HEE*
...!!!
AHEM!
AAAH! FINALLY! HAND 'EM OVER, ELF!
SILENTLY, SKYWISE OBEYS AND...
BRRR! PICKNOSE, YOU IDIOT! SHUT THE DOOR!
BATDUNG! THE KING DID CHEAT! THE EMBARRASSMENT! THE DISGRACE!
IF THE ELVES FIND OUT, WE'LL NEVER LIVE IT DOWN!

OH, PICKY...!
DON'T MOVE!
ULP!
WH-WHY?
'CUZ I CAN THROW THIS A LOT FASTER THAN YOU CAN RUN!
...ER...UM ...*FRAZZ*...
SO THE RING WAS RIGHTFULLY BEARCLAW'S ALL ALONG, EH?
AND YOU'VE BEEN HOLDING CUTTER UNJUSTLY ALL THIS TIME!
I CAN'T WAIT TO TELL MY WHOLE TRIBE --
NO! YOU MUST SWEAR NEVER TO BREATHE A WORD OF THIS!
MY KING'S A CHEAT, BUT IT'S MY DUTY TO PRESERVE A SEMBLANCE OF HIS HONOR.
I HEAR YOU, TROLL...BEEN THERE, MYSELF. WHAT'LL YOU GIVE ME IF I SWEAR?
THE RING OR THE LAD - PICK ONE. MY BUTT'LL GET HAMMERED, ANYHOW!
"CHOOSE!"
WHEW! HARDER THAN I THOUGHT!
BEARCLAW CHARGED ME TO GET THE RING. IF I CHOOSE CUTTER, I FAIL IN MY TASK!
AND AFTER...IF I BREAK MY VOW TO PICKNOSE AND TELL --
-- CUTTER WILL HATE ME FOR BEING DISHONEST. BUT IF I DON'T TELL... *SIGH* HE'LL STILL HATE ME --
-- FOR FREEING HIM AGAINST HIS WI
AND WORD.

SHORTLY...
GULP *MUNCH* I TELL YOU...
DECEIT AND GUILE, M'DEAR ...THE ONLY WAY TO STAY ON TOP!
CLEVER MUNGY-WUNGY! OF COURSE, A MAIDEN SUCH AS I --
-- KNOWS NOTHING OF DECEIT! YOU CAN ALWAYS TRUST LITTLE, OL' ME!
GITCHY GITCHY GITCH...
HOO HOO HOO HEEE HEEEE
SLAM!!
GASP!
WHAT...?? I FINISHED STACKING THE POTS!
SHUT UP! NO QUESTIONS!
DON'T GIVE ME ANY TROUBLE!
WHAT'S GOING ON...? STAY BACK!!
SPURB!!
AAACK!!
NO YA DON'T!!
UNH!!

UURGH!
WHY'D YOU HAFTA WAIT 'TIL NOW TO FIGHT BACK?
COWARD!
YOU'RE ALL COWARDS AND BULLIES!
IN THE SACK! QUICK!
WHY?! WHY ARE YOU D -- MMRRF?!
'CUZ YOUR SILVER-HAIRED CHUM'S BARGAIN YOU OUT OF HER FERRET!
HAH! THAT TIES YOUR TONGUE, I SEE!
THOUGHT YOU'D IMPRESS US? PROVE SOMETHIN'? PARADE OUT-SIDE, SOMEDAY, TO OUR APPLAUSE?
CHUH! DREAM ON!
THAT FRIEND O' YOURS GOT THE ROTTEN END OF THE DEAL, THOUGH. I'D HAVE PICKED THE RING, FOR SURE!
SULKIN,' EH...? YOU JUST DO THAT --
-- QUIETLY!
HEY! LOOKS LIKE ONE POKIN' BIG BEDTIME SNACK, THERE! YOU AUTHORIZED...?
ER...
ORGY IN THE MINERAL BATHS...KING'S ORDERS...
GOTTA GO!

GROWL MAY I BE DOOMED TO LIVE ABOVE GROUND BEFORE I EVER GET MYSELF MIXED UP WITH YOU POINT-EARED VERMIN AGAIN!
TRUDGE
TRUDGE
TRUDGE
WHIIINNE!
SPLISH!
SPLASH!
CREEE-EEEAK!
WHISSSSSSHH!
BLAPP!
MMMPH!

C-CUTTER...!
YOU... YOU'VE GROWN!
HIGH ONES...! I MISSED Y --
-- THIEF!!
WHAM!
UUUH!

WHAT -- OOOW!! WHAT D'YOU M -- ?!?
-- YOU STOLE MY HONOR!!
YOU MADE ME BREAK MY WORD!!
BAF!
UUNH! *OOUF!* BUT... BUT...YOU'RE FREE -- !
RIGHT! AND NOW THE TROLLS ARE SURE ALL ELVES ARE SELF-SERVING SNEAKS!
GASP I TOLD YOU BEFORE ...IT'S NOT THAT POKING SIMPLE!
MMMH MMMH MMMMM?
I'M THAT SIMPLE!
I HATE MEAN TRICKS!
I HATE BENT TRUTHS!
AAAAAGH!

I HATE SNEAKS!
SPLUJTCH!
COUGH *COUGH*
YOU MIGHT AS WELL STILL B BLINDFOLDED!
SPLAT!
MY CHIEF SET ME A TASK!
UUUH!
BECAUSE OF YOU--
-- I FAILED!

THAT'S ALL YOU CARE ABOUT!!
ROCK SKULL! YOU DON'T KNOW --
SPLOSH!
-- SKYWISE! YOU JUST CARE ABOUT SKYWISE!
AND YOU JUST CARE ABOUT --
-- HOW WE LOOK TO THE TROLLS!
WHO GIVES AN OWL PELLET, YOU HIGH-HEADED DREAMER?!
GET DOWN HERE WITH THE REST OF US!!
UNGH!

FWIPP!
NO!!
PLASH!
I DREAM OF SLASHING THROUGH HATE AND LIES!
I DREAM OF HOW IT COULD BE - EVERYONE LIVING AS ONE!
TROLLS AND HUMANS, TOO? THAT DREAM'LL GET YOU KILLED!
I WON'T LET YOU *UUUNH!* WHATEVER IT TAKES... I'LL KEEP YOU SMART *RRGH!* AND ALIVE!
WHY?!
BECAUSE I --

TAM...!
...FAHR!

THE MOMENT STRETCHES...THE RAIN STOPS...
OH...
SO...
SO THIS IS WHAT --
-- IT FEELS LIKE...!
A CHOICE IS MADE...
YES.
NOW WE BOTH KNOW!
AACK!
HA HA HAH HA HA!

SOON...

LOOK! IT'S CUTTER! HE'S BACK!

AYOOOAAH!

HOW IN FREEFOOT'S NAME...?!

THANK THE HIGH ONES!

LONG INTO THE NIGHT...
BECAUSE OF THE TROLLS, WE HAVEN'T MUCH TO WELCOME YOU HOME WITH, JUST NOW.
BEING WITH MY TRIBE IS EVERY-THING!
EVEN SO, THINGS ARE REALLY GONNA CHANGE AROUND HERE, NOW YOU'RE BACK, CUB!
THIS'LL COST YOU EIGHT AND TWO KNIVES...SIX SWORDS AND THREE EIGHTS OF ARROWHEADS!
SLURP
YES, INDEED! *HENH HENH*
WHAT WAS IT LIKE, DEEP IN THE TROLL CAVERNS?
BEARCLAW NEVER TELLS US ANYTHING!
I DON'T KNOW.
"THEY TOLD ME TO STAY BLIND-FOLDED AND I DID."
PA-TOOF!
ICK!
A SON OF MINE OBEYED TROLLS?!?
THE WHOLE TIME YOU WERE DOWN THERE, YOU DIDN'T NOSE AROUND?
UH UH.
DIDN'T STEAL ANYTHING?
UH UH.
DIDN'T MAKE TROUBLE OF ANY KIND - EVER?
NOPE.
JOYLEAF... YOU SURE THIS IS MY CUB?

YOU'RE TRULY *BRAVE*, LOVEMATE.
DID YOU GET ALL THOSE *BRUISES* FROM FIGHTING THE TROLLS?
NOPE... FROM *CUTTER!*
WHAT?!
TELL YOU *LATER*.
GIGGLE IN THE *DREAMBERRY PATCH?*
WELLLL... IF YOU'RE NOT *TOO BUSY!*
SKYWISE... WHATEVER SECRETS REMAIN, THE MATTER OF THE RING IS CLOSED.
YOU *DIDN'T FAIL!* SOMETHING PASSED BETWEEN YOU AND *CUTTER*, I KNOW...
...SOMETHING *WONDROUS*.
ALWAYS STICK BY HIM. *PROMISE*.
YOU DIDN'T EVEN NEED TO *ASK*, MY CHIEF.
HELLO, *FROSTY-MANE!* WHERE DID YOU *GO?*
FOR THE FIRST TIME IN A YEAR, THE STARGAZER LIES BACK, CONTENT...KNOWING MORE OF LIFE, NOW, THAN HE EXPECTED...KNOWING MORE OF **SHARING** IN IT THAN HE EVER HOPED.
WHY? *CHUCKLE* *MISS ME?*

AND...
SCARED...?
WHY?

YOU SAID... RECOGNITION'S... TOO MUCH RESPONSIBILITY.
YES, I DID

BUT, FROM THE MOMENT I SAW YOU BORN, I - I KNEW YOU.
I GUESS I'VE ALWAYS KNOWN --

-- OUR SOULS ARE TIED! WE'RE ...WE'RE...
DON'T TRY, TAM.

THERE'S NO NAME FOR YOU AND ME... UNLESS...

...UNLESS IT'S "BROTHERS..."
YES... BROTHERS --

-- IN ALL BUT BLOOD.
THE END

THE LOVE OF BROTHERS...OF FAMILY...OF TRIBE...THE BEDROCK OF THE WOLFRIDERS' EXISTENCE IS ONCE MORE AT RISK...
ALL IS NOT AS WELL WITH THE HUMANS AS HOPED. THEIR DRUMS OF DEATH SOUND A RENEWED, INTENSE ANIMOSITY... THEIR HUNTING PARTIES SEEK, WITH CHILLING SINGLENESS OF PURPOSE, THE HEART OF THE ELVES' DOMAIN...
THAT POUNDING... LIKE THUNDER...! LIKE WHEN THE SKYFIIRE BOILED THE BLOOD IN MY VEINS!
RUM TA-TA-TUM TUM TA-TA-RUM
WHAT DOES IT MEAN, FATHER?
IN THE WEEKS THAT FOLLOW, IT BECOMES CLEAR...

THE HUMANS' RELENTLESS SEARCH FORCES A FATEFUL DECISION...
YOU THINK IT'S THE RIGHT THING TO DO?
SIGH IIT'S NOT AS IF THERE'S NO COMING BACK.
AND IT DOESN'T MEAN THE HUMANS HAVE WON, BELOVED.
WHEN HE CAN CHOOSE, THE WISEST WOLF PICKS FLIGHT OVER FIGHT.
AH, JOYLEAF...! EVEN IF IT IS FOR THE BEST, I COULDN'T MAKE THAT CHOICE...
...WITHOUT YOU!
THIS TIME, WE'LL DO IT DIFFERENT! WE WON'T WAIT FOR THE HUMANS TO FIND US.
WE'LL FIND A NEW HOLT, BEYOND THEIR REACH.
BUT THIS IS OUR HOME! WHY SHOULD WE HAVE TO LEAVE?!
FOR NOW IT'S BEST WE FIND A FRESH LIFE SOMEWHERE FREE OF THIS BLOOD-FEUD.
THE FATHER TREE WILL STAND, AWAITING OUR RETURN, NO MATTER HOW LONG IT TAKES.
WHO SEARCHES WITH ME...? STRONGBOW...?
WHEN YOU SEND FOR US, WE'LL GO WHERE YOU LEAD.
FOR NOW, I'LL STAY TO GUARD THIS HOLT... AND MY NEW CUB.
AAA! AAAWAAAH!
SOFTLY, LITTLE DART.

BUOYED BY BEARCLAW'S OPTIMISM, THE HUNTING PARTY SETS OUT WITH A SENSE OF ADVENTURE.
I AM SO PROUD OF YOU, BELOVED.
HEH HEH THERE IS SOMETHING TO STARTING ANEW, EH?
ANY HOLT WILL BE HOME AS LONG AS WE'VE NEW CUBS TO RAISE.
BE FUN AT LEAST TRYING, EH, FOXFUR?
FOR MANY DAYS AND NIGHTS THE HOLT-HUNTING PARTY TRAVELS, COVERING A LARGE SWATH OF TERRITORY.
THEN... ONE NIGHT... A FORBIDDING STENCH TAINTS THE BREEZE.
PHEW! WHAT'S THAT?
BEARCLAW FEELS HIS GREAT, BLACK WOLF BRISTLE BENEATH HIM.
SNIFFING, LISTENING, PEERING AS ONLY THEY CAN, THE ELVES DETECT A WATCHING PRESENCE.
BUT ALL THEIR FOREST-BORN SKILLS REVEAL...
...NOTHING.
ONLY ONE THING IS SURE -- IT IS NOT THE SCENT OF MAN.
WHATEVER THIS FOULNESS IS, BLACKFELL KNOWS AND FEARS IT.
THAT'S ENOUGH TO RAISE MY HACKLES.

SHORTLY...
A CUB! FRESH KILLED... AND FOR THE PLEASURE OF IT!
THE KILLER IS NEAR, BELOVED, I SENSE IT.
SLASSH!
AAAAIIIEEE--
CUTTER STANDS FROZEN WITH SHOCK...
CUTTER!!
AND THEN, WORSE HORROR...
...THE MONSTER SENDS!
BLOOD AND FIRE, CAT AND SNAKE JOINED BY TWISTED, ANCIENT MAGIC!

A BURST OF SHEER HATRED, NAUSEATINGLY INTENSE!
RRRRAAAAAAAARRRRR!!
HATRED THAT SUDDENLY TURNS, LOOMING DARKLY OVER A HELPLESS BEARCLAW.
HIGH ONES...! CAN'T ...FACE IT!
AAYOOOAH! RUN!
RUN FOR YOUR LIVES!

SOMETIME LATER, AS MINDS TOO SHATTERED TO "SEND" RECOVER...
JOYLEAF!
ANSWER US, SISTER!
FOXFUR!
JOYLEAF! BELOVED! WHERE ARE YOU?!
STONE-STILL AND SILENT... HE SENDS.
AND SENDS.
AND...
M-MOTHER... IS SHE--?
EVEN IF SHE WERE UNCONSCIOUS... SHE WOULD HAVE ANSWERED ME BY NOW.
NO! WHY SHOULD YOU GO AFTER THAT MONSTER ALONE?
WE ALL HAVE A RIGHT TO AVENGE OUR DEAD!
JOYLEAF WAS MY SISTER, REMEMBER?

I DECIDE WHAT RIGHTS ARE YOURS! I AM CHIEF!
IN THE END, ONLY ONE DEFIED HIM... THE ONLY ONE WHO COULD.
THE OTHERS MUST GO BACK, BEARCLAW, I AGREE.
BUT I'M COMING WITH YOU!
YOU CAN'T STOP ME!
WE HAVE MADE A CUB, BELOVED, WHO IS ALL WE ARE...
... AND MORE.
EITHER DO AS I SAY... OR SEND ME TO JOYLEAF'S SIDE!
I DON'T CARE WHICH!
FROM NOW ON, MY SHINING DEHL, HE SPEAKS FOR US BOTH!

FATHER AND SON CANNOT ASK THEIR WOLF-FRIENDS TO FACE PREY SO HORRIBLY UNNATURAL.
NIGHTRUNNER! BLACKFELL! STAY THERE!
DIMLY AWARE OF CUTTER'S NEW TONE OF COMMAND, BEARCLAW BEGINS THE HUNT.
DAYS PASS. FAR BEYOND THE BORDERS OF THE WOLFRIDERS' TERRITORY, THE TRAIL REMAINS PLAIN.
MORE THAN MERELY SCENTING THE CREATURE, BEARCLAW FEELS ITS EERILY INTELLIGENT MALICE...
HE KNOWS, AS ONE CUNNING MIND TO ANOTHER, THAT IT ONLY TOYS WITH THEM...
... DRAWING THEM ONWARD, EVER AND ALWAYS, JUST OUT OF REACH.
IN THE SILENCE BETWEEN THEM, BEARCLAW SENSES HIS SON'S CONCERN.
BUT TO SPEAK, EVEN TO SEND, NOW, WOULD BREAK THE SPELL THAT DRIVES HIM ON...
...WHEN HIS SPIRIT WOULD OTHERWISE CRUMBLE.
AT LAST, DEEP IN AN UNEXPLORED PART OF THE FOREST, BEARCLAW VEERS OFF THE MORE OBVIOUS TRAIL...

...FOLLOWING HIS REVENGE-HEIGHTENED INSTINCTS TO A HIDEOUS DISCOVERY...
...MADCOIL'S EMPTY DEN!
THE SMELL TELLS ALL... BUT HE MUST SEE FOR HIMSELF.
CHOKE ...FOUL AS DEATH IN HERE
F-FATHER... HUMAN BONES!
THEY'VE SUFFERED FROM MADCOIL'S ATTACKS TOO!
DEEPER BACK IN THE REEKING DEN, BEARCLAW DOES NOT HEAR.
FOR HIS LAST SHRED OF HOPE, HELD AGAINST ALL REASON, IS...
...GONE.
MY BELOVED... MY SOUL... I'VE HAD SEASONS ENOUGH!
"SOON... SOON... I WILL JOIN YOU!"

SO PITIFUL...
SO TENDER...
SO *FINAL*...
...IS THE WHITE GLEAM OF BONE NEWLY LAID BARE.

BUT SOMETHING ELSE REMAINS...

...THE MOST *PRECIOUS PART* OF HER SHE COULD HAVE LEFT BEHIND.

...AND BEARCLAW WILL DO WHATEVER HE MUST...

...TO *SAVE* THAT.

FOR LONG, TORTUROUS HOURS THEY LIE IN WAIT FOR THE MONSTER'S RETURN.
BUT EVEN THE FIRES OF REVENGE CANNOT OVERCOME YOUTHFUL EXHAUSTION.
IT IS AS BEARCLAW WISHES.
HE KNOWS WHAT HIS SON DOES NOT...
THAT THE CREATURE WHO LIES IN THE DARK WOOD, COILED AND MOTIONLESS...
...WANTS ONLY...
...HIM.

SO... YOU KNOW I'VE BEEN *WAITING* FOR YOU, EH?
MOCKING... CHALLENGING...!
YES... *YES, CURSE YOU! I'LL COME!*
TAM...
I COULD HAVE DONE A *BETTER JOB*...
...OF SHOWING HOW I *LOVE* YOU.
WHEN *YOU* HAVE CUBS OF YOUR OWN... DO *BETTER*.
DO *BETTER*.

EVEN AS THE WOLFRIDER CHIEF STRIDES TOWARD HIS FATE...
...HE STRUGGLES TO THROW OFF THE CREATURE'S INSANE MIND-TOUCH.
BUT NOTHING PREPARES HIM...
...FOR HIS FIRST FULL SIGHT...

...OR THE DARK INTUITION THAT THE MONSTER'S SUPERNATURAL HATRED IS SOMEHOW...

...FAMILIAR!

INSTANTLY, NEW IMAGES ASSAULT HIS MIND.
HE SEES!
HE SEES HOW HATE, HABITUAL AND UNREASONING, AWOKE THE STAGNANT POOL OF MAGIC...
...AND GAVE IT LIFE!
LIFE BENT ON THE DESTRUCTION OF ITS OWN CREATORS!
JOYLEAF... RAIN... AAH...!
EYES-HIGH... SHALE... SNAPPER... CRESCENT...
MY FAULT... ALL OF IT!
GAARRRHHHH!!!

AND SEEING, HE UNDERSTANDS WHY HE COULD NOT FACE THE MAGIC-BORN MONSTROSITY BEFORE.
MY... FAULT...
SLOWLY IT SLITHERS TOWARD WHAT SEEMS AN EASY KILL.
BUT THIS IS BEARCLAW!
SNAAARRRLL
EEEEEEYOOOWWLLL!
THUKK!
HAAAIIIEEEEE!!!

TWELVE HUNDRED YEARS HE HAS LIVED...
TWELVE HUNDRED YEARS OF INGRAINED CUNNING, SKILL AND EXPERIENCE...
WHISSHH!
TWELVE HUNDRED YEARS FACING THE BEASTS, THE ELEMENTS AND THE HUMANS...
RRIPP!
GASP!
SPLUTCH!
IN THE "NOW" OF WOLF-THOUGHT, HE FIGHTS AS NEVER BEFORE...
...WITH BUT ONE PURPOSE!
GRRRR-GURGL-RRR!
EEEYOOOOWRRRRRR!!!!

HHHHISSSSSSS!
HEH TO WIN MY JOYLEAF, I LET A BEAR EMBRACE ME ONCE.
YES, THAT'S RIGHT. YOU'RE MINE! I MADE YOU!
CHOMP!
SHRAKK!
AND NOW WE BOTH PAY -- AAAAAAGH!!
FWISSH!
UUNGH!
UUUUUURRRRGH!
K-THUDD!

I HURT IT... BAD...!
ALMOST ENOUGH...!
ENOUGH, BELOVED...! REST!

BEARCLAW!
COUGH *COUGH*

FINISH IT FOR ME... TAM, MY CHIEF-SON...
...TAKE... NEW MOON.

YOUR HAND IS MINE NOW...!

WHEN YOU STRIKE... I WILL STRIKE... TOO...
I SWEAR IT, FATHER!

WE'LL FINISH IT TOGETHER!

TO DIE AND STILL BE IS THE WAY OF THINGS FOR OUR KIND.
I REMAIN... AND AWAIT THE COMPLETION OF MY ATONEMENT.
BLACKFELL, LOYAL WOLF-BROTHER, YOU BEAR MY HUSK AWAY.
TAKE STRENGTH FROM IT... EAT... DRINK...
...THAT WE MAY RUN TOGETHER FOREVER.
OUR CUB'S A SMART ONE, DEHL. HE SUMMONS THE TRIBE.
YES, OLD BADGER. HE HAS LEARNED... FROM BOTH OF US.
BUT THE ONE WHO'S LIKE A SON... HIS PAIN'S DEEPEST OF ALL.
FORGIVE, MY GOOD ARCHER. TRY... TRY NOT TO HATE.
AYYYOOOOOAAAAHHHHHH!
HAH! A GOOD HOWL! I COULD NOT ASK FOR A BETTER FAREWELL!
YOU SEE, GRENN? YOU WILL ALWAYS BE REMEMBERED...
...AND LOVED.
THE CHIEF'S LOCK SUITS HIM.
CHUCKLE WE ALWAYS KNEW IT WOULD, DIDN'T WE, SWEET?

THAT'S IT, SON! I'VE USED MANY A WEIGHTED NET AGAINST A RAGING BEAR.
IT IS MORE THAN THE BINDING OF A NET HE HAS BEGUN... IT IS THE BINDING TOGETHER OF THE TRIBE.
WELL, WELL! THERE'S A BIT MORE OF ME IN HIM THAN I THOUGHT!
NOW, TAM, MY CHIEF-SON! BY THE HIGH ONES, NOW!
NOW!
BEARCLAW! JOYLEAF! GUIDE ME!
YOUR HAND IS MINE! STRIKE!
SHRIEEEEKKKK!!

YOU DID IT, LAD! RIGHT THROUGH THE EYE!
MADCOIL IS FINISHED!
IF ONLY THE REST OF THE MESS I LEFT BEHIND COULD BE TIDIED SO QUICKLY.
MY SON, AT LEAST YOU TRY... HAULING MADCOIL'S HEAD THROUGH THE FOREST AT GREAT TOIL...
...LEAVING IT AS A MESSAGE OF PEACE...
...TO SHOW THE HUMANS THEY'RE SAFE FROM THE EVIL THEIR SHAMAN AND I, TOGETHER, CREATED.
BUT STILL THEY MISUNDERSTAND.
< WHAT DO WE DO WITH IT? >
< BURN IT! >
< GOTARA'S SACRED FIRE WILL RID US OF THIS ABOMINATION! >
< THEN, ONE BY ONE IF NEED BE... >
< ... WE WILL COMPLETE THE DESTRUCTION OF THOSE WHO CREATED IT! >

SIGH
HATRED OUTLIVES ITS CREATORS.
YOU HAVE NO CHOICE, MY SON.
AYE, BELOVED. THIS LESSON SEARS MY SOUL.
< MY CHOSEN ONE SHALL BE AVENGED AS NO OTHER HAS! >
SO IT GOES, ROUND AND ROUND...
< TABAK! TABAK! MY MAN IS DEAD! *SOB SOB* >
< WE WILL CLEANSE THE LAND WITH FIRE! >
< THE WILL OF GOTARA SHALL BE DONE! >
ROUND AND ROUND...

LONG AGO, I SET HIS FEET AND MINE UPON THIS PATH.
AND ONE WHO SUFFERED DEEPLY FOR MY FOOLISHNESS...
GOTARAAAA... !*
THUKK!
...NOW BRINGS IT FULL CIRCLE.
WHERE WILL OUR TAM'S PATH TAKE HIM, DEHL?
WHEREVER IT LEADS, BELOVED...
...WE WILL BE THERE... ALWAYS...
...ALWAYS...

VOLUME